THE ABC's of Wellness for TEACHERS

An A–Z guide to improving your well-being in the classroom and out

by Teena Ruark Gorrow,
Susan Marie Muller,
and Kappa Delta Pi

Kappa Delta Pi,
International Honor Society
in Education

Indianapolis, Indiana

Kappa Delta Pi, International Honor Society in Education
3707 Woodview Trace, Indianapolis, Indiana 46268-1158

Printed in the United States of America

08 09 10 11 12 5 4 3 2 1

ISBN 978-0-912099-47-7

Direct all inquiries to the Director of Publications, Kappa Delta Pi, 3707
Woodview Trace, Indianapolis, IN 46268-1158.

Executive Director	Series Editor	Design and Layout
Faye Snodgress, CAE	*Karen L. Allen*	*Chuck Jarrell*
Director of Publications	Assistant Editor	Cartoonist
Kathie-Jo Arnoff	*Kathy Murray*	*Benita Epstein*

To order, go to *www.kdpstore.org.*
Quantity discounts for more than 20 copies.

Library of Congress Cataloging Publication Data

Gorrow, Teena Ruark, 1958-
    The ABC's of wellness for teachers : an A–Z guide to improving your
well-being in the classroom and out / by Teena Ruark Gorrow, Susan Marie
Muller.
        p. cm.
    Includes bibliographical references and index.
    ISBN 978-0-912099-47-7 (pbk.)
    1. Teachers—Health and hygiene—United States. 2. Teachers—Job
stress—United States. 3. Teachers—Time management—United States. 4.
Stress management—United States. I. Muller, Susan (Susan Marie) II. Title.
    LB3415.G67 2008
    371.1—dc22

                                                                    2008038206

About the Authors

Teena Ruark Gorrow is an Associate Professor of Education and Interim Director for the Elementary Education Program in the Department of Teacher Education at Salisbury University in Maryland. She earned her doctorate in Education Policy, Planning, and Administration from the University of Maryland College Park and holds an Advanced Professional Certificate with the State of Maryland in administration, teaching, and school counseling. Dr. Gorrow served 17 years as a public school teacher, assistant principal, principal, central office supervisor of instruction, and district coordinator of special programs. During her eight years as a college professor, she has instructed undergraduate and graduate courses in classroom management, education foundations, and cooperative learning; coordinated the region's professional development schools program; and supervised field-based teacher interns. Dr. Gorrow is a member of Kappa Delta Pi and former Counselor of the Rho Eta Chapter.

Susan Marie Muller, Professor of Exercise Science at Salisbury University, is a Certified Health Education Specialist and a Certified Health-Fitness Instructor through the American College of Sports Medicine. She earned her doctorate in Health Education from the University of Maryland College Park and has 26 years of teaching experience. Dr. Muller holds an Advanced Professional Certificate with the State of Maryland in Health and Physical Education, and her work includes program review, curriculum development, and standards revision for the accreditation of teacher preparation programs in School Health Education. Dr. Muller serves as a lead reviewer and auditor of American Alliance for Health Education (AAHE) Specialty Reports for NCATE accreditation and is a member of the Board of Directors for AAHE, the Standards Revision Committee, and the AAHE/NCATE.

Acknowledgments

Kappa Delta Pi Publications would like to thank the following individuals who shared their expertise in producing this book.

Reviewers

Kevin Adams	John J. Franey	Jennifer Osborne
Ann M. Baker	Lindsay Johnson	Charisse Willis

Teena Ruark Gorrow would like to acknowledge the following individuals: Wayne Dennis Gorrow; Ellen Parks Ruark; Paul Kenneth Ruark; Paula R. Gibb; Ernest B. Beath, III; and James Gibb.
Susan Marie Muller would like to acknowledge the following individuals: Ted Green; Karen A. Muller; and Katie M. Muller.

Table of Contents

Sidebars

Extras

References 79

Suggested Resources 82

About This Book

Passionate about positively affecting lives, teachers strive to be a source of hope for those who might otherwise be hopeless. Teachers tirelessly prepare engaging lessons for diverse populations, work evenings and weekends to catch up on piles of paperwork, take phone calls from parents at home, and attend evening programs. In addition, teachers answer to many stakeholders and serve in numerous and varied roles throughout their schools. Being everyone a teacher needs to be takes energy.

Because teaching is a time-consuming profession that can drain energy, and because today's teachers are tremendously busy people with lives and families outside of school, staying in balance poses a serious challenge. Though attending to your own wellness may not be as easy as ABC, using this book to enhance your well-being and gain tips on improving your habits is. Just as easily, you can find suggestions for your classroom, encouragement toward a healthy balance in your life, and potential solutions to concerns. Whether you are an intern, a beginning teacher, or an experienced professional, these ABC's were written to help you be the well teacher you want to be.

As you explore *The ABC's of Wellness for Teachers*, watch for these icons—they flag important information:

 **Pick up a quick tip about personal wellness.**

 **Get advice from experienced teachers.**

 **Read the inspirational words of professionals.**

What Is Wellness?

In the Report of the 2000 Joint Committee on Health Education and Promotion Terminology published by the American Association for Health Education (AAHE), wellness was defined by AAHE/ AAHPERD (2001, 103) as, "An approach to health that focuses on balancing the many aspects, or dimensions, of a person's life through increasing the adoption of health enhancing conditions and behaviors rather than attempting to minimize conditions of illness."

Essentially, wellness is an expanded concept of health that incorporates the idea of fully living one's life with meaning and vitality. Today's wellness is about achieving a higher state of being. Though the discovery and development of wellness is unique to each person, the Six Dimensions of Wellness, as presented by the National Wellness Institute (2007), provides an interdependent model for discussion and includes emotional, intellectual, occupational, physical, social, and spiritual components. Explore these dimensions and other matters related to your wellness, alphabetically or randomly, in the pages of *The ABC's of Wellness: An A–Z guide to improving your well-being in the classroom and out.*

Acceptance

Teachers share a universal language in which they voice philosophical comments such as, "I believe all students can learn," and "I work diligently to create a learning environment conducive to the individual needs of my students." These types of remarks illustrate willingness to recognize and accommodate students' diverse needs. Yet, teachers often do not accept their own successes and missteps.

Does this scenario sound familiar? You planned the perfect instructional day, but things sped downhill when the school's server failed and students could not log onto the computers. You tried to salvage the lesson, but without the technology needed, outcomes were not met. During the next class session, you miscounted while assigning students to cooperative groups and presented the wrong manipulatives for the guided activity. Chaos reigned and worsened with each passing minute.

STUFF HAPPENS

Things don't always go as planned! It happens to every teacher— veteran to preservice—and usually at the worst possible moments. Your overall success is affected by your willingness to take inevitable situations in stride. When you can accept that your best-laid plans went awry, you will find it less stressful to move on to Plan B. Replaying disappointing events in your mind, focusing on flaws, and calling yourself names only makes you feel miserable and undermines your confidence.

Be careful of blowing mistakes out of proportion. Shift your focus from what went wrong and feelings of failure to accepting what happened, brainstorming strategies to prevent recurrence of those problems, and developing effective ways of managing similar situations in the future. Though the growing pains you endure in these situations require a healthy dose of reflective if-that-ever-happens-again decision-making, through them you gather a repertoire of strategies for adjusting mishaps in progress. Be patient with yourself—students aren't the only ones who learn when you teach. Also see **Attitude**, **Believing in Yourself and Others**, and **Flexibility**.

Imperfection can be a marvelous thing! Stellar minds have created amazing inventions due to mistakes! For example, we wouldn't have those helpful little sticky notes had it not been for a failed attempt to develop a strong adhesive. Imagine our loss if that mixture had been discarded because it didn't turn out the way it was planned. Nobody's perfect; but the way you perceive your mistakes can predict your future success.
Teena Gorrow, *ABC's of Wellness* coauthor

Advocacy

There will be times when you will need to serve as an advocate for yourself, others, a group of people, or an organization. Unfortunately, society is filled with people who seemingly feel better by belittling others. Some of these individuals may have lunch with you in the teacher's lounge or be assigned to your grade-level team.

Hearing disparaging remarks is likely to generate an emotional response in you that either stirs a desire to support the belittled or causes you to feel stressed. Whether you speak up on behalf of the offended will depend on your willingness to become involved, as well as the situation in which the encounter occurs. The best course of action is to decide whether a response from you at that time is appropriate. If so, develop a short, positive, and accurate rebuttal. Though it might not be an easy thing to do, your advocacy can protect someone's reputation, make you feel better about yourself, and redirect the entire discussion toward the positive. On the other hand, if you decide that speaking up is inappropriate, avoid participating in the discussion and physically remove yourself from the situation. Be aware that if you remain with the group or individual making the negative comments, your silence can be interpreted as agreement.

Apologize-ability

Did you overreact, snap at a student, insult a colleague, or ignore a friend's need? If so, apologize. Did someone offend you, and then offer an apology? Accept it! As much as possible, strive to live in peace with those around you, even when you believe you are in the right. There are lots of lonely, but correct people out there—don't be one of them. Nurturing a grudge due to conflict with others is damaging to those relationships and your overall well-being. It can even impair your ability to concentrate and sleep restfully. From a wellness perspective, it is best to swallow your pride and quickly get over it (see **Forgiveness**).

Appearance

Those famous people on the glossy magazine covers pay professional makeup artists, fashion designers, and photographers to make them look fabulous. Rather than moaning about your imperfections or focusing on your flaws, reject stereotypical generalizations about beauty. Comparing your self-image to retouched and air-brushed pictures imposes unattainable standards that lead only to your dissatisfaction. Assess your strengths and needs for a look that makes you content. Your outward appearance can be a reflection of how you feel about yourself and, ultimately, affect the way you conduct yourself. If you decide that you need some help pulling it together, visit a salon for a makeover. Evaluate what you can or are willing to change, and accept the rest.

Dress for success and occupational wellness.
Career advisors suggest that employees dress for the position they hope to have five years in the future. Professional colleagues, parents/guardians, administrators, and board members will make initial decisions about you based on your outward appearance. Be aware that your professional reputation includes your appearance, and that relates to your wellness at work (refer to **Occupational Wellness**). Whether you dream of being a school administrator, guidance counselor, or career teacher, dress professionally every school day. Even when your school sponsors a fund-raising event that, with a donation, allows you to dress down, keep professional. Wearing jeans with holes, dirty sneakers, and a well-worn college sweatshirt isn't the best image to project. Clothing that is too tight, too loose, or too short is also inappropriate. Consider wearing black jeans for a casual, yet professional look.

Dressing for occupational wellness includes appearing professional to your students. Teens are consumed by appearance and even preteens are quick to notice style. Though students may remark on how you look and apply their standards to your appearance, you should develop your own professional style and avoid dressing to fit in with students or appeal to their standards.

Attitude

Consider Maria, a nontenured second-grade teacher who secured a position in the school of her dreams, but soon learned that budget cuts and decreasing enrollments were forcing the school district to cut teaching positions. Though she would still have a teaching position, a teacher with seniority would transfer to Maria's classroom next year. Maria is understandably heartbroken to be displaced from her dream position, but her name is first on the list for the next opening, and she knows that one of the second-grade teachers in her school is retiring. Maria told friends that despite leaving her current grade level, she is happy because it looks like she will have a job next year in the same school and at the grade level she desires most.

Rather than focusing on what she would lose, Maria adopted a positive attitude and focused on the position to which she could be reassigned. She chose to be happy and thankful, instead of complaining to others. How do you generally react to unexpected and disappointing circumstances? How do your responses affect your attitude? How does your attitude affect others around you?

Negative attitudes deplete energy, waste time, stir up unpleasant physiological reactions in your body, and strain your relationships with others. On the other hand, positive attitudes encourage vitality, hope, and creativity, and they are contagious. Even in bleak or unfair situations, look for the positives, focus on opportunities, and choose a good outlook. Try not to flip-flop as the situation changes—upbeat and hopeful today, but discouraged tomorrow. Choose to stay positive. You may lack control over some circumstances, but you really can control your reaction to them.

Very few situations are inherently stressful. Your attitude is a decision you make. Girdano, Dusek, and Everly (2005) suggested that an individual's interpretation of life events is what generates a stress response. So, if you essentially become what you think, imagine the possibilities! For emotional and physical dimensions of wellness, avoid a pessimistic focus on problems, and look on the bright side of situations affecting you.

Attitude + Positive = 7.5 Years

They've done the math at Yale University, and optimistic people were found to live 7.5 years longer than those with a gloomy outlook! Incredibly, having a positive attitude was ranked as more important than lower blood pressure and cholesterol levels. It seems that when people perceived themselves as living in a state of chronic stress, their cellular aging increased, which literally subtracted years from their lives (Lewine 2005). You don't have to be a researcher or mathematician to figure this math: Add "choose a positive attitude" to your to-do list.

Balance

As defined by AAHE/AAHPERD (2001, 103) in the *American Journal of Health Education*, wellness is "An approach to health that focuses on balancing the many aspects, or dimensions, of a person's life through increasing the adoption of health-enhancing conditions and behaviors rather than attempting to minimize conditions of illness."

By this definition, then, staying in balance is more than eating well and exercising. It's about attending to your personal care and juggling responsibilities in healthy ways to achieve a complex, higher state of being. Balance facilitates your ability to fully live your life with vitality and meaning. If you spend substantial time focusing on one area of life, you can neglect other areas and become out of balance, like a car spinning out of control on an icy road.

"I CAN'T SEEM TO GET OFF THE GROUND."

Think of your wellness dimensions as a mobile (see graphic below). Each decision a human being makes affects the whole being, similar to the way a tug on one arm of a mobile moves the entire mobile.

How balanced are your dimensions of wellness?

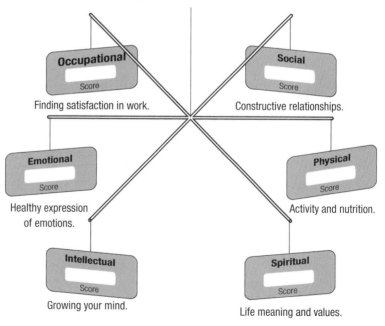

Occupational / Score	**Social** / Score
Finding satisfaction in work.	Constructive relationships.
Emotional / Score	**Physical** / Score
Healthy expression of emotions.	Activity and nutrition.
Intellectual / Score	**Spiritual** / Score
Growing your mind.	Life meaning and values.

(Graphic © 2008 Gorrow and Muller)

Pulling one dimension immediately affects the whole and the mobile becomes imbalanced, which eventually can chip away at the stability of other dimensions and take a toll on your overall well-being.

Yet, there are times in life when one event may take precedence and create imbalance. Perhaps it is preparing to teach a new grade level, finishing a graduate degree, caring for a sick relative, starting a family, or getting divorced. One major event can require so much of your attention that taking care of other responsibilities seems impossible. Striving for balance comes down to what you value and how you prioritize your time.

Take some time to reflect on your life while looking over the Balance vs. Imbalance table and completing the wellness assessment in the **Extras** section (see page 73). Remember that you can support your overall wellness by developing balanced involvement of each of the dimensions; but if any one of these components is left unattended, the whole becomes disrupted (Hahn, Payne, and Lucas 2007).

Believing in Yourself and Others

Do you expect your students to conduct themselves appropriately or act poorly for the substitute teacher? When you prepared them for your absence, did you focus on what they should not do or thank them in advance for supporting a visiting teacher, indicating confidence in their willingness to be successful? Did their behaviors match your expectations?

Students tend to achieve what their teachers expect them to achieve, otherwise known as self-fulfilling prophecy. In her review of research regarding teacher expectations and attributions on student performance, Jeanne Ellis Ormrod (2006) highlighted studies showing that students use their awareness of the teacher's treatment to draw inferences about the abilities of self and others, create self-perceptions, and alter behaviors.

Self-fulfilling prophecy and wellness

Finish the following sentences to check how self-fulfilling prophecy could be affecting your students' wellness.

- In general, I think that my students _____

  _____

- My students generally perform _____

  _____

- I expect my students to _____

  _____

- My students probably think I believe that they _____

  _____

- Regarding their performance, my students probably think I believe

  _____

- My students probably think I expect them to _____

  _____

Now consider beliefs you have about yourself and your performance. Belief in yourself, or self-efficacy, involves your perception of your ability to perform various tasks and to overcome difficulties associated with mastering a given task (AbuSabba and Achterberg 1997). Are your perceptions working for you?

Most of us tend to select tasks or activities in which we believe we can succeed and avoid those we believe might lead to failure. Sometimes we miss wonderful opportunities because we think we can't or that someone else thinks we can't. Self-efficacy is a potent predictor of many health-related and career-enhancing behaviors, and it is influenced by past performance, vicarious experience, and the encouragement received from others (Karren et al. 2006). Stopping to examine your beliefs about yourself and your students, explore missed opportunities, and create or revise goals could be beneficial. Recording moments of inspiration and revelations in a journal or sketchbook helps track progress.

So, what do you believe? Maybe you need to revamp your thinking so that you hold high, yet reasonable expectations. Don't settle for status quo. Enhance self-efficacy by taking on more daunting tasks with the assistance of a colleague, friend, or students. Once you experience some success, moving forward and achieving higher-level goals becomes more likely. Success breeds success. See **Acceptance** and **Attitude.**

Body Image

Body image is the way you see your physical self, including all aspects of your appearance. It is a multifaceted concept that refers to a person's perceptions and attitudes about his or her own body, particularly but not exclusively its appearance (Cash and Pruzinsky 2002). Research suggests that your body image can affect your feelings and self-esteem, which influence your behavior and wellness (Gorrow, Muller, and Schneider 2005).

- How do you see yourself in terms of body size?
- How often do you feel good about other aspects of your physical appearance, including your hair, facial features, shoulders, and complexion?
- Is your view of your body image healthy and accurate?
- How does your view contribute to your feelings and self-esteem?
- Are your expectations reasonable?
- Do your feelings and expectations set you up for unhealthy behaviors?
- Do you need to make adjustments?

Body Mass Index (BMI)

No discussion on wellness, especially in light of the obesity epidemic in the United States, would be complete without mentioning the need to achieve a healthy, realistic weight for your body size. One measurement tool commonly used to evaluate body size, based on height and weight measurements, is Body Mass Index (BMI). The Centers for Disease Control and Prevention (2007) identified three BMI categories based on measurement scores: Normal Weight is 18.5–24.9; Overweight is 25.0–29.9; and Obese is 30.0 and above.

Calculate your BMI

A commonly used formula for calculating BMI is body weight in kilograms divided by height in meters squared, or BMI = kg/M^2. To calculate your BMI, take your weight in pounds and divide by 2.2 to get your weight in kilograms. Then, take your height in inches and multiply by 0.0254 to get your height in meters and square this number. Lastly, divide the kilograms by the meters squared to get your BMI score. Learn more about BMI and calculate your score online at *www.cdc.gov/nccdphp/dnpa/bmi/index.htm*.

Percentage of body fat

Many people are concerned about their percentage of body fat compared to lean or nonfat tissue. Health risks tend to increase as the body fat percentage exceeds 25 percent for males and 32 percent for females. In general, most non-athletes should strive for a body fat percentage of 12–25 percent for females and 5–18 percent for males. Note that healthy amounts of body fat differ for men and women, and also vary to some degree for athletes and occupational requirements (Howley and Franks 2007).

Note: Consult a health professional when setting and maintaining your personal weight goals. Your target weight must be one that is right for you, given your particular health and genetic makeup, and not necessarily one posted on a chart in a doctor's office, book, or on the Internet. Some measurement scales, for example, may not accurately account for competitive athletes, people with muscular bodies, or nursing mothers.

Breathing Techniques

Imagine that you have been the advisor of a prestigious school organization for years. No one else on the faculty would take on this daunting task because of the huge investment of time required and extracurricular activities involved, especially with no stipend. However, you were willing to serve and appreciated the importance of the organization to your students. This year, a stipend will be given for the leadership role, so several people have stepped forward and you must apply to be considered. You are exasperated, thinking that your years of effort were both unnoticed and unappreciated.

Everyone experiences moments of sheer frustration, irritation, or feelings of being overwhelmed. Things happen that just aren't fair, logical, or reasonable. When you sense your emotions taking control, breathe deeply, focus on being calm, and refuse to fly into a rage or offer remarks you will later regret.

Breathing techniques frequently are used to control stress. Belly breathing, in which a person relaxes the chest and allows the stomach to go in and out with each breath, generates less arousal of the sympathetic nervous system, causing a greater relaxation effect than thoracic breathing where emphasis is on chest movement (Seaward 2006). So when you feel stressed, take a moment to breathe slowly, focusing on using your stomach, rather than your chest.

Choices

One's philosophy is not best expressed in words; it is expressed in the choices one makes . . . and the choices we make are ultimately our responsibility.
Eleanor Roosevelt, First Lady 1933–1945 and
civil rights advocate

Decisions, decisions . . . Which dessert should I pick—low-fat or the one I really want? How should I differentiate instruction for this topic, and what form of assessment would be best for follow-up? I am sure that was a bruise on Josie's cheek, so do I call Social Services, report it to the guidance counselor, or wait to see what happens?

Teachers probably make 1,000 decisions a day. Some choices are simple and others heart-wrenching with professional or legal implications. Regardless of the nature of alternatives you face daily, the power to choose is usually yours. While you will not always have much time to think through potential solutions, these problem-solving suggestions may help you make a good choice when time is on your side.

- Clearly identify the issue that requires your decision.
- Brainstorm potential choices and ask for others' opinions when appropriate.
- Dissect choices to identify potential strengths and weaknesses.
- Eliminate choices that would go against your values and beliefs.
- Consider policies or legal mandates that might limit your possible choices.
- Determine whether your emotions are involved. Feelings change so take care not to make unwise decisions based on them.
- Present your idea as concisely as possible when the choice requires an announcement to others, and allow them to ask questions or share their views.
- Reflect on success and barriers.
- Decide whether other actions are required.

Classroom Management

No book on teacher wellness would be complete without mentioning classroom management, because poor classroom management skills contribute to stress. Managing your classroom is more than simply having a theoretical plan for dealing with student discipline. It also includes creating a positive learning community, planning and conducting effective lessons, using time efficiently, developing rules and procedures, organizing materials of instruction, effectively managing paperwork, communicating with students and their families, and managing your work habits. Furthermore, developing caring and supportive relationships, providing opportunities for meaningful participation and bonding, teaching life-skills, and setting high expectations build resiliency for students and teachers, and resiliency is important for long-term wellness (Henderson and Milstein 2003).

You will find helpful hints and tips on this important topic in *The ABC's of Classroom Management* (Kramer 2005), published by Kappa Delta Pi. For more information, see page 83.

Commitment

Commitment refers to having a sense of purpose and meaning in your relationships and life in general. Being committed requires you to become actively engaged in your work and to follow through on your responsibilities to fulfill your purpose. Commitments reveal your values through the goals and ideals that you seek and drive your behaviors (Blonna 2007). As a teacher, you dedicate yourself to serving others as a part of your values system. Some days it will take sheer determination and grit to persevere through the mounds of paperwork and concerns about student performance. Maybe that's why teaching has been referred to as a work of heart. Just remember—no guts, no glory. Don't give up. Being steadfast in your resolve to make a difference in children's lives increases your own sense of purpose.

Give 100 percent of yourself to your students and profession from 8 a.m. to 4 p.m. Keep evenings for you and your family. When you must take work home, keep it to a minimum. Your children and spouse also need your attention. In turn, you will be renewed by their love.
Glenda Watkins, 1988 Kansas Teacher of the Year

Communication

Communication with others is an important part of bringing together all the components of wellness. In general, communicating well involves three different skills: initiating, listening, and responding.

- Initiating is sending a message, often called encoding (Blonna 2007), and can be verbal or nonverbal, and involve posture, position, facial expressions, or body language. It is wise to pay attention to the nonverbal signals that you send to others.

- Listening well reduces conflict and increases the likelihood of developing the caring relationships required for increasing resiliency in the classroom. Improve listening skills with these tips:
  o Stop what you are doing when someone begins speaking to you.
  o Maintain eye contact.
  o Nod occasionally, or utter "uh-huh" in agreement.
  o Ask a question for more information if needed.
  o Avoid planning your response while the person is speaking.
  o Check your posture—it suggests your openness to the conversation. Uncross your arms and legs.

- Responding skills are used to ensure that the message was received or to request further clarification. Paraphrasing what was said to make sure you heard the message correctly is one of the most effective responding skills. Begin paraphrasing with an opening line such as, "So what you are saying is . . . " or "Your perception is that . . . ." For additional information, use open-ended statements such as, " Tell me more" or "That's interesting" to continue the conversation.

Conflict

Consider the following example: Two of your students argued in the cafeteria and a teacher assistant brought these agitated youths to you to help them resolve their disagreement. At the same time, you have been anxious all day about whether to register for the upcoming administrator's certification exam. You are apprehensive about a move to the main office because you enjoy teaching. Where do you begin to resolve these conflicts and how might they impact your emotional wellness?

Internal and external conflicts can cause anxiety. Let's examine potential steps you could use to resolve this conflict:

- Talk it out.
  o Listen to what the teacher assistant has to say.
  o Allow each student to share his or her point of view.
  o Acknowledge each student's feelings.

- o Focus on the immediate problem and clarify what is causing the turmoil.
- o Determine whether others are needed to resolve the conflict.
- Identify associations between what is creating the anxiety and the desired outcome.
  - o Resolving the conflict between the students first is the obvious desired outcome in this situation.
  - o Resolving the anxiety about becoming an administrator while handling the student concern would be the secondary desired outcome. Without a doubt, administrators deal with various conflicts at multiple levels, among them student-to-student, teacher-to-student, teacher-to-teacher, teacher-to-parent, and central office administrators. This teacher probably was weighing the rewards of being an administrator against leaving teaching, while feeling some pressure to make an occupational decision.
- Allow time to calm down if the conflict has become elevated or very emotional; separate students a few minutes while you think.
- Create a plan of action for resolution or negotiate solutions.
  - o Seek win-win solutions.
  - o Encourage compromise.
  - o Avoid assigning blame to allow everyone to save face.
  - o Summarize agreed-upon solutions to ensure student understanding.
  - o Monitor student progress.
- Get help from a mentor teacher, administrator, or guidance counselor if needed.
- Enroll in a conflict resolution class or other professional-development activity to help you meet these everyday challenges, improve your skills, and build your confidence.

D Diet

Yes, diet is a four-letter word and, of course, you've heard, "You are what you eat." But did you know that what you consume can pep you up or bring you down? Your body is a complex mixture of chemicals and each time you eat, you add something to that mix. Be vigilant in the school cafeteria and wary in front of the snack machine; nibbling on that treat can contribute to a lack of energy later.

Many snack foods are high in simple sugars, which are digested and absorbed very quickly, resulting in a sharp rise in blood insulin levels. Insulin is a hormone that allows the blood sugar, glucose, to enter various cells of your body. A sharp rise in insulin usually results in a rebounding low blood glucose level. Because the brain relies on blood sugar for smooth functioning, low blood glucose results in feelings of fatigue and a loss of mental focus. Insulin also is responsible for increasing the storage of fat in adipose cells. Therefore, those pick-me-up snacks actually add excess body weight and leave you feeling tired.

Maintaining a balanced diet is essential for achieving high levels of wellness. For suggestions on balancing your diet, visit *www.MyPyramid. gov* (United States Department of Agriculture 2007), where you will find 12 different dietary models. After reviewing the specific recommendations, you'll need to decide on the best diet for you. You also may want to review **Physical Wellness**.

Dropping Out

- Do you talk about your principal in the lounge or gossip in the hallways?
- Would any of your personal behaviors at school be characterized as overly aggressive or shy?
- Do you mentally check out, drifting in and out of conversations?
- Are you usually at least a few minutes late to meetings?
- Do you check your Blackberry®, talk on the cell phone, knit, grade papers, or write greeting cards during faculty meetings?
- Do you undermine others or draw attention to yourself in professional gatherings?

Answering yes to any of these questions could mean that you are exhibiting dropping-out behaviors. As this list shows, dropping out is not limited to physically removing oneself from the situation. It is possible that you feel unappreciated, bored, uninspired, unenthusiastic about the task at hand, or that you have suffered a huge disappointment professionally. If this represents your situation, consider the following strategies to fight dropping-out behaviors.

Anti-dropping-out strategies

- Be aware that you are exhibiting dropping-out behaviors.
- Examine your feelings and emotions.
- Reflect on your behaviors and their effects on others.
- Analyze options to address issues that you identify.
- Take steps to change your behaviors.
  - Talk with a mentor or trusted friend.
  - Brainstorm solutions to school problems with teachers on your team, and consider sharing with the school improvement team.
  - Stop yourself before making negative remarks about a colleague. Do not gossip!
  - Volunteer for a leadership role that requires you to report progress during meetings.
  - Engage rather than disengage in decision-making activities.
  - Be on time for professional obligations, even if you think they are a waste of time. Instead of showing disrespect, you could advocate fewer meetings and more frequent e-mail discussion.
  - Skip grading papers or knitting during meetings. Such behaviors are rude and unprofessional, and you would not allow students to behave that way during your instruction.

Emotional Intelligence and Feelings

Goleman (1995) defined emotional intelligence as the ability to feel and express the full range of human emotions. He suggested that, while society places great value on intelligence quotient (IQ) scores, emotional intelligence actually plays a larger role in determining a healthy life or one prone to disease. Learning to identify and resolve feelings can help prevent many types of disease. Similarly, the ability to monitor and use emotions to guide thinking and actions can help increase work productivity and overall happiness (Hales 2007).

Fear, worry, a negative self-image, and unrealistic expectations commonly block the development of emotional intelligence. Avoiding pain and blaming others also hinder emotional intelligence. When caught in these emotions or habits, individuals often act in ways that decrease chances for successful outcomes. Have you ever felt upset by an e-mail message from a student's parent or hurt not to be invited to an after-school gathering celebrating a colleague's birthday?

These are legitimate feelings, but concentrating too much on your feelings about a situation brings misery and places too much emphasis on a given circumstance. Furthermore, you become physiologically and emotionally upset by letting these feelings control you and make things worse with inappropriate responses. Controlling one's emotions and resulting behaviors is essential for maintaining caring relationships and success at school. Remember that feelings are always subject to change!

To increase your emotional intelligence, become aware of your emotions. Reflect on them, think through potential behavioral responses associated with your emotions, focus on displaying your emotions in socially acceptable ways, and consider others' feelings. Developing emotional intelligence increases social competence and the pleasure others derive from having you as a friend or colleague.

Emotional Wellness

Emotional wellness includes:

- being aware of and accepting your own and others' feelings;
- feeling positive about yourself and your life;
- expressing and managing feelings;
- accepting responsibility for your actions;
- coping with stress;
- realistically evaluating your limitations;
- forming trusting relationships;
- appreciating support from others; and
- approaching life with an optimistic attitude.
  (National Wellness Institute 2007)

In general, emotional wellness recognizes your capacity to effectively manage and communicate your feelings. It is not about suppressing your emotions, pretending that they don't exist, or allowing them to control you. Rather, it is about realizing that everybody has feelings, that everyone experiences a wide range of emotions, and that those emotions are subject to change. The trick is knowing when and how to appropriately display your feelings.

How is your wellness on the job?

Signs of optimal emotional wellness for teachers include:

- being in touch with and accepting your feelings;
- working through negative emotions with a trusted mentor or colleague;
- recognizing circumstances that trigger emotions;
- managing feelings to maintain professional demeanor on the job;
- demonstrating professional dispositions in your overall approach to teaching;
- setting a positive, emotionally healthy classroom tone; and
- accepting students' feelings and accommodating diverse needs.

Environment

"NOW KAYLA, DO I NEED TO EMPTY OUT YOUR DESK TO GET YOU TO ORGANIZE THAT MESS?"

Your environment, ranging from your personal space to your living area, work environment, and eventually to the world beyond, contains a wide variety of substances that ultimately impact your health. You have the most control over exposure to pollutants within your work and living spaces. These pollutants include light, noise, dirt, and microorganisms. Does your classroom support good health? Is it clean, organized, and appealing? Does it inspire creativity and promote a positive learning environment? You and your students need a healthy living space. Clean! Reorganize, tackle overdue piles, recycle paper, and discard outdated materials. Dust your desk and bookshelves, straighten storage areas, have students clean their desks, and open the windows for fresh air. For related information, see **Occupational Wellness** and **Social Wellness**.

Expressing Yourself in Words

You know that speaking negatively of your students and colleagues is unprofessional and potentially damaging. What about how you talk about yourself and your abilities? Do you view self-deprecating language as being humble or funny? Which words do you utter when describing your professional performance? Take a look at the following two well buckets—"banks" of words—to identify words you use most often to describe yourself.

Optimistic Self-Talk

• Qualified	• Cheerful	• Pleasant
• Capable	• Successful	• Positive
• Confident	• Thriving	• Talented
• Willing	• Able	• Happy
• Enthusiastic	• Eager	• Lighthearted
• Proficient	• Skilled	• Encouraged
• Effective	• Accomplished	

Pessimistic Self-Talk

• Inexperienced	• Hopeless	• Failure
• Inept	• Poor	• Weak
• Awkward	• Unskilled	• Bungling
• Weak	• Amateurish	• Incapable
• Powerless	• Sloppy	• Clumsy
• Unqualified	• Defeated	• Thoughtless

Are you surprised by your words? Others view you as the expert on all there is to know about you. If you say, "I'm terrible in math," others will believe that your mathematics skills are weak and not count on your ability. When you convey confidence in your ability, others will place hope in your skills. Besides hurting your reputation, negative self-talk defeats your efforts before you begin. We tend to believe what we hear—even when we say it about ourselves.

What if there's truth in your negative words? It may be time to make changes. Are you ready? Use tips throughout this book to improve your outlook and wellness habits. A good place to begin might be **Goal Setting**. Are you too hard on yourself? Look intentionally for your positive attributes and affirm your accomplishments. Words have power! See **Acceptance**, **Attitude**, **Believing in Yourself and Others**, and **Your Words Are Powerful**.

Fear of Failure or Rejection

If you have experienced major life changes, you are probably familiar with the pangs of fear. Physiologically, fear occurs when a signal sent from the hypothalamus to the pituitary gland sets off the "fight or flight" response, causing a rapid rise in heart rate, breathing, and sweating. Although this survival response is designed to assist you in dangerous situations, it can be activated when no real threat exists. In non-life-threatening events, this response can trigger inhibiting reactions, rather than adrenalin-motivated positive actions.

How did you respond the last time your principal entered your classroom for an unannounced observation? Did you confidently invite him to join your lesson or hear yourself trip on the words you were saying to the class as your heart rate kicked into high gear? When fear attacks in non-dangerous situations, thoughts of failure or rejection are usually the culprits. Fear of failure involves acceptance and protecting your self-image, while fear of rejection relates to your perception of how others view and accept you. The good news is that positive interactions with colleagues, students, parents, and administrators over time will help decrease the anxiety associated with change, uncertainty, doubt, or intimidation. Instead of imagining how many things can go wrong as you face the situation producing your fear, calm down, practice effective breathing techniques, visualize your success, and do your best. See **Acceptance**, **Attitude**, **Breathing Techniques**, and **Visualization**.

Dealing with anxiety

- Recognize that everyone makes mistakes, including you.
- Admit your shortcomings.
- View stressful situations as learning experiences.
- Examine and evaluate anxiety-producing events to determine causes.
- Adjust future behaviors to encourage success.
- Apologize if you erred; it will strengthen relationships and enhance wellness.

  (Blonna 2007)

Note: These tips are not intended to replace consultations with a health professional. If you are experiencing ongoing anxiety, depression, intense sadness, worry, or other intense emotions, you are encouraged to talk with your doctor. Also see **Worry**.

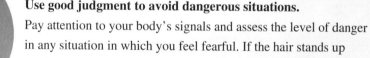

Use good judgment to avoid dangerous situations.

Pay attention to your body's signals and assess the level of danger in any situation in which you feel fearful. If the hair stands up on the back of your neck or you have that strange feeling in your stomach, don't be too quick to pass it off as unfounded. Schools are like other public places in terms of necessary safety precautions, so pay attention to those around you. Know school procedures for dealing with unruly students, and avoid positions where you could be injured. For example, avoid crouching down beside an angry student when trying to calm that student. It places you in a position where your legs are unstable, and you must look up at the student who could easily strike or spit on you. Carry your cell phone when you report for duties, and have office numbers on speed dial. Use good judgment when walking to and from your vehicle, and schedule after-school working time when you know others will be in the building. If you must schedule late conferences, arrange them when an administrator can be present. Also see **Safety**.

Flexibility

You were desperately counting on the planning block during first period to prepare materials for the day's lessons. You planned to copy student handouts, organize manipulatives, and grade tests. Then the intercom interruption stopped you in your tracks: "Excuse me, Miss Smith. The music teacher had to leave school for an emergency and we have no one to cover your special. There will be no music class today." You inwardly groan as you grasp the reality of losing 45 minutes you so greatly needed in order to cover music period with your class, though you know nothing about music—not to mention that you are at this instant unprepared for your entire day. You wish you had called in sick.

Thinking on your feet is vital to being flexible. Though this situation is not ideal, getting upset or taking it out on the students will not solve your problem. Most teachers experience unwanted and unexpected changes beyond their control, usually with little notice. Being flexible—going with the flow—is the best way to handle unforeseen circumstances. As mentioned in **Acceptance**, it is good practice to have a back-up Plan B for such occasions. A resource file of extra activities and special lessons can turn a predicament into a spontaneous, even fun, learning event.

Go with the flow.
Consider the "mind like water" concept martial artists teach. Picture a stone tossed into a pool of water. As the stone drops into it, the water reshapes and adapts to the force, dissipating it to return quickly to its original calm. The water does not anticipate or ignore the stone, but responds to it when needed and only as much as necessary. When stones are tossed into your pond, try to emulate the water being parted by the stone (Insel and Roth 2008).

Focus

Focus on what really matters to you. Don't allow your life and expectations to become anything but deeply personal reflections of what matters the most to you.
David Niven, social scientist and psychologist

Pay attention. Please focus! How many times do we issue these reminders to students? Yet we need to pay attention too. You are devoted to a time-consuming occupation that easily can zap your time and energy. So it's important to heed other dimensions of wellness besides occupational. As discussed in **Balance**, focusing primarily on one dimension causes an imbalance that can become a serious threat. Be sure to assess your balance using the resources in this book (see **Balance**, **What Is Wellness?**, and **Extras**), and then focus on the dimensions of your wellness that need attention. You can't be all things to all people, as the saying goes, so focus on what matters to you.

Me, multi-task?

We live in a fast-paced world, and demands placed on us can seem overwhelming. To be most productive, we often focus on multiple tasks simultaneously, believing that "multitasking" is to our benefit. Sometimes it works well; other times we endanger ourselves and others. We talk on cell phones, check messages, coordinate our children's after-school activities, and gulp down a fast-food breakfast, all while driving in rush-hour traffic. But wait! The overall quality of our efforts can decrease while stress levels increase, and we may experience the physical symptoms of spreading ourselves too thin. As our attention spans sprawl, forming and maintaining strong interpersonal relationships can be more difficult. Human bonds are sustained mostly because an individual takes time to focus on another human being to discover the unique qualities that attract and bind them together. As we allow increasing distractions into our lives, the bonds we form with others become more tenuous.

Though at times we must multitask, habitual multitasking is a symptom of being too busy, out of focus, or out of balance, especially if this behavior prevents us from enjoying vacation or down time. If this habit sounds familiar, pay close attention to what you do by performing your tasks in a focused manner for one week. Then evaluate your performance. Assess the efficiency and quality of your work. Are you more organized? How does it feel to complete one task at a time versus constantly multitasking? Often an intentional decision to focus increases work quality and decreases stress levels.

25

Forgiveness

The weak can never forgive. Forgiveness is the attribute of the strong.

Mohandas Gandhi, political leader and philosopher

Something happened. Your have hurt feelings and can't believe the way you were treated. The more you think about the offense, the more upset you feel. Caution: Danger ahead. If you let bitterness grow in your heart, resentment will take root and begin to control your emotions. Eventually, these feelings will preoccupy you and negatively affect your relationships and health. Forgive. Let go of blame and regain a sense of control over your life, behavior, and personal actions. Recognize that your perception of any event represents only one side of the story, which is never totally free from bias. Though not easy, forgiving a person who offended or disappointed you is vital to your own wellness and even may influence physical healing (Karren et al. 2006).

Here's what forgiving can do for you:
- Reduce anger and hostility.
- Release you from bondage and guilt.
- Open the door to restored relationships.
- Remove blame.
- Open your mind and allow creativity to flow.
- Help you regain a sense of control.
- Restore inner peace, confidence, and hope.

P.S. Just because you want to pursue forgiveness doesn't mean that the person who offended you will be like-minded. Forgive your offender anyway, and then let it go.

Germs

IT'S OKAY TO OBSESS ABOUT HAND WASHING

If you came down with chicken pox as it spread through your classroom, bent over to tie a kindergartener's shoe only to have him sneeze in your face, or tried to move a nauseous student's test materials just in time, you can write your own blurb on germs. They are everywhere and teachers make great hosts for these pesky critters!

Teachers may fall prey to childhood diseases in their adult years from contact with contagious students and can count on routine exposure to nasty colds and the flu each year. Practicing these habits will reduce your chances of getting sick:

- Frequently wash your hands and teach students to do the same, especially before lunch and after restroom breaks.
- Model appropriate behaviors like covering a cough or sneeze, and then washing hands.
- Request a "large box of tissues" on your student supply list each year for classroom use.
- Keep a hand sanitizer available at your desk.

Goal Setting

Setting goals identifies priorities and helps you accomplish more. To get started, try the SMART principle to structure Specific, Measurable, Attainable, Realistic, and Time-specific goals (Conzemius and O'Neill 2006). Consider applying SMART to your wellness goals. Begin by analyzing the dimensions of wellness through assessments and other information presented in this book. Think about your reflections, responses to questions, and assessment scores to identify areas in which you are doing well and areas that could use improvement. Then develop a few short- and long-term goals for maintaining successful areas and improving your low-scoring dimensions of wellness. Develop a routine for checking your progress, and remember to reward yourself for achieving your goals. Consider engaging in goal-setting discussions with a colleague or friend for support, future reinforcement, and social wellness.

Get the goods on goals.

- Get the big picture—identify what needs work. Brainstorm with colleagues about academic programs, relationships with students, classroom management concerns, and professional development.
- Using the SMART principle, list 3 to 5 goals for each area identified.
- Distinguish between short- and long-term goals, and eliminate any that seem unrealistic.
- Prioritize goals in order of importance to you.
- Identify potential costs, required materials, and time commitment.
- Create an action plan.
- Examine your progress and adjust goals.
- Reward your progress.

Habits

Do you head for your car during your planning period to sneak a cigarette, or substitute a snack and grading papers in place of your opportunity to eat lunch and relax a few minutes? Do you put off all your school work until Sunday evening and then dread trying to complete everything? Though some habits can be wellness-enhancing, some of your habits could be reducing your ability to maintain high levels of wellness. Examine your daily habits and set personal goals to replace poor behaviors with more healthy habits. See **Goal Setting**.

Negative Habit   **Goal**

Hobbies

What is your leisurely pursuit? Whether you sing, read, walk, fish, bicycle, jog, play a musical instrument, crochet, dance, or weed a garden, pick a pastime to amuse and distract you from the regular grind of responsibilities. Take time from your routine daily to do something you enjoy—for balance and to attend to each dimension of your wellness. A hobby does more than provide an outlet for tension or an area of enjoyment. It can nurture several dimensions of wellness.

Walking, for example, contributes positively both to your physical dimension of wellness through activity and exercise and to your spiritual dimension when you reflect on values and enjoy the sites around you while walking. Walking can even add to your intellectual dimension of wellness if you listen to an audio-book or podcast and to your emotional dimension if you mentally work through a stressful issue. A simple walk adds to your social dimension when you enjoy it with others and to your occupational dimension when your work requires physical fitness or you plan instructional activities while walking.

Humor

A politician, attorney, teacher, and student were all passengers on an airplane that was about to crash. However, there were only three parachutes. The attorney looked at the others with dismay and said, "Many people count on me for help." He grabbed the first parachute and jumped out of the plane. Immediately, the politician said, "I'm the smartest and most necessary person employed by our local government." She snatched the second parachute and jumped out. Looking intently into the eyes of the student, the teacher tenderly said, "I see the potential in you, and I know that you are going to do great things with your life. You take the last parachute." The student replied, "That's okay, Miss Jones. There are still two parachutes—the smartest and most necessary person employed by our local government just jumped out with my backpack."

Humor, laughing, and having fun seem to be lacking in some of today's classrooms. In fact, some teachers still subscribe to the old adage, "Don't smile until Christmas." Yet, laughing is a source of satisfaction. According to Charles (2000), students are drawn to smiling teachers, and smiling has been shown to be contagious (Wild et al. 2003). You do not have to be a stand-up comedian to lighten the mood in your classroom; but when funny things happen, it's okay to laugh—as long as it is not at the expense of a student.

Students enjoy a good laugh, and developing a sense of humor also can make you feel better physically (Gorrow 2004). Positive physical effects of laughter include improving immune system function, relieving stress, suppressing stress hormone production, relieving pain, and relaxing muscles (Karren et al. 2006). Laughter also has a positive influence on neuroendocrine hormones (Lefcourt 2001) and restores physiological homeostasis (Seaward 2006).

Imagination

Your imagination can be your gateway to realizing a high level of personal well-being. What you see in your mind's eye can powerfully

30

impact your mental and emotional health. Dreaming, or creating scenarios in your mind, inspires creative solutions and new possibilities and expands your options, all of which lead to enhanced feelings of well-being. So, dream big and let your imagination lead you to a higher level of wellness. Also see **Visualization**.

I learned this, at least, by my experiment: that if one advances confidently in the direction of his dreams, and endeavors to live the life which he has imagined, he will meet with a success unexpected in common hours.

Henry David Thoreau, American author

Intellectual Growth

The brain is an integral network of connections among neurons that is constantly reshaped by experiences. According to Rosenfield (1988), we constantly reshape everything that enters the brain and assign new meaning. Therefore, intellectual growth involves not just knowing things, but also reworking, reclassifying, and generalizing information in various new ways. You are a professional in a demanding career that requires you to have ideas and solutions. Grow your mind! Attend professional conferences, read journal articles related to your content, network with colleagues, and incorporate new ideas into lesson plans to help you and your students stay interested and motivated. Learn from those around you, including your students.

Intellectual Wellness

Intellectual wellness includes:
- incorporating stimulating mental activities into your daily life;
- being creative;
- expanding knowledge and abilities;
- sharing your skills with others;
- taking advantage of learning resources available within and beyond the classroom;
- cherishing opportunities to learn and expand knowledge;

31

- actively challenging your mind;
- reading; and
- staying engaged with current issues.
  (National Wellness Institute 2007)

In general, intellectual wellness involves actively engaging in stimulating mental activities to expand knowledge. It's about being open to new ideas, critically analyzing information, and creatively problem-solving. An intellectually well person not only uses available resources to facilitate his or her learning, but is eager to serve as a resource by sharing knowledge with others.

How is your wellness on the job?

Signs of optimal intellectual wellness for teachers include:
- being a life-long learner;
- pursuing creative instructional techniques instead of formulated lessons;
- engaging in professional reading and writing activities to expand knowledge;
- attending conferences to learn and share knowledge with others;
- assessing student performance to inform instructional decisions;
- using research to guide curricular development; and
- making real-world connections to the classroom.

Journal Writing

Reflecting on your life and recording your thoughts in a journal can be a valuable way to enhance your wellness. Journaling:
- lets you privately review past events and thoughts about the future;
- provides emotional catharsis (emptying emotional reserves through expression);
- frees your mind to focus on other emotions and tasks;
- helps you map out future courses of action;
- gives you a format to examine important life events;
- offers flexible expression—you can sketch, doodle, or write; and
- helps you see your personal progress.

Journaling isn't limited to thoughts on paper. You can express yourself in blank books or through online blogs and scrapbooks.

Joy

Focus on the journey, not the destination. Joy is found not in finishing an activity but in doing it.
Greg Anderson, author and lung-cancer survivor

Imagine being presented two boxes, both beautifully gift-wrapped with glittering bows and ribbons. One, however, bulges on all sides with joy, while the other is packed tightly with joylessness. Which box would you choose?

Choosing the box of joy is a no-brainer. Yet, life doesn't post signs announcing the potential outcome of each decision we make, helping us see results as obvious as those two gifts. How often we unwittingly select misery over bliss! Too easily we overlook experiences that would bring enjoyment because they seem obvious or mundane.

Do you remember being comforted as a child after falling off your bike? Can you recall a loved one's proud cheer when you marched across the graduation stage? Back then, did you endure family meals even though you preferred to be out with friends? What do you notice when you walk your dog? How often do you feel impatient while driving to work?

These commonplace moments weave the fabric of your life quilt, yet are easily dismissed as unimportant. You have people to love, animals to pet, sunrises to view, hugs to give and receive, and students to amuse you— unless you are too busy, too miserable, or too gloomy to notice. Decide to appreciate and cherish good things in your life.

Joy enhancers:
- Find pleasure in ordinary things.
- Dream while awake.

- Use your five senses—listen to the birds chirping after the alarm sounds, savor the taste of your food, smell the rain, feel the sand between your toes, watch a baby sleep.
- Hug people you love and let them hug you.
- Watch the sun set until it is out of view.
- Help others out of genuine kindness, rather than a guilty conscience.
- Share your talents and encourage others who want to learn what you know how to do.
- Sleep.
- Choose to be happy now. Don't put off happiness until summer break, retirement, marriage, divorce, having children, or sometime in your future.

Joy kidnappers:

- Complaining
- Hating
- Gossiping
- Comparing
- Coveting
- Fearing
- Worrying
- Whining
- Arguing

Kindness

What do you remember about your favorite teacher? How well he or she knew the content? Likely you remember the way the teacher treated you. What do you hope your students remember about you?

Teachers are like farmers. The seeds we plant determine the harvests we reap. What we sow in the lives of those around us will one day come back into our own lives. Helping or giving to others enhances our self-esteem, relieves stress, and improves our psychological well-being. Volunteers often report a surge of well-being, often labeled "helpers' high." They gain a positive sense of self-worth, along with a unique calmness and warmth associated with helping others (Hales 2007). Sowing kindness seeds is as simple as expressing interest in students, offering help, or just listening. Empathy cultivates relationships with colleagues, too.

Locus of Control

Psychologist Julian Rotter defined locus of control during the 1960s, and revealed that individuals with an internal locus of control were healthier overall than those with an external locus of control (Seaward 2006). People with an internal locus of control believe that they possess the faith, willpower, and confidence to influence the outcomes of their actions, while those with an external locus of control believe outside influences such as luck, nature, or other people are in control. Studies have shown that individuals with an internal locus of control are more independent and optimistic about their future than those with an external locus (Hales 2007). The big idea: Take control of your life—believe that you can influence the outcomes in your life.

Medications in Your Desk

Plagued with the occasional nasty migraine, Mrs. Nelson created a toiletries kit that included her prescriptions and placed it in her bottom desk drawer. Several weeks later, when a terrible headache threatened to turn into a migraine, she reached into her toiletries kit for her prescription, only to find that her medications were missing.

Your desk is frequently unsupervised, such as when you walk with students to other locations. Unlike makeup or deodorant, medicines can have a tempting appeal. Find a private place for medicines that you can keep under lock and key. Reminder: let the nurse supervise administration of all student medications, adhering to school district policies to avoid potential legal implications.

Mentoring

Teaching can be very challenging, and far too many teachers leave the profession because of pressure or unexpected responsibilities.

Being effective in classroom management, planning, organization, and communication, however, leads to well-being and success in the classroom. How do you ensure your effectiveness and avoid becoming an I-left-teaching-statistic? Support.

The art and science of teaching requires a very real learning curve, and when we try to figure out everything on our own, we wind up feeling alone. Yet we aren't, thanks to mentor teachers who lovingly share their time, patience, and best practices. Support can be a classroom or e-mail away when you know on whom to rely for assistance.

You might benefit from a mentor if:
- You are a new teacher or an experienced teacher in a new school or grade level.
- You have difficulty planning or delivering instruction.
- You need support with a new responsibility you accepted.

Schools with formal mentoring programs assign mentors; but if your school does not provide mentors, ask your principal to identify a teacher who can guide your way. Principals have insight into faculty members' performances and abilities, and they assign extra duties, so they are in the best position to match someone to your needs.

Make the most of your time with a mentor.
Participating in activities with your mentor lessens feelings of isolation, builds skills, and improves job satisfaction. You might:
- meet each week to share concerns, ideas, rubrics, and units to build teacher readiness;
- plan instruction for individual lessons and units;
- develop assessment tools and rubrics;
- interpret data and assess impact on student learning to modify instruction;
- network with their professional acquaintances;
- co-present a topic of interest during a faculty meeting or professional conference;
- engage in team teaching or co-teaching activities;
- set goals for professional development;

- observe your mentor's classroom for tips on student behavior management, record-keeping, organization, and transitions between activities; and
- ask your mentor to observe your teaching to provide feedback for improvement.

Connecting with a mentor can change your approach to work and significantly affect your occupational wellness by impacting your self-confidence, attitude toward teaching, and overall performance. Experienced teachers might consider being a mentor for someone else.

Niche

Your wellness includes finding your place in life, your identity. Besides knowing who you are and what you are meant to do with your life, having a niche gives you a sense of belonging and knowing that others care for you. How's your niche at school? Do you fit in? If you feel isolated or invisible, you may find these tips helpful.

- Be friendly and offer upbeat greetings to others.
- Be approachable when a colleague comes to your door.
- Co-teach or take a field trip with another teacher on your team.
- Join a committee to help the school and to meet other faculty members.
- Attend after-school functions to cheer on your students and meet parents.
- Invite your team to lunch in your classroom.
- Socialize occasionally during break instead of working in your classroom.

Also see **Mentoring**, **Occupational Wellness**, and **Social Wellness**.

No's Are Not Always Negative

Spend time with a small child, and you soon discover that *no* still exists in the English vocabulary. Though constant no's from a child quickly get old, you might long for the freedom of using that one-syllable protective device. When was the last time you actually said no and held your ground?

Did you say sure, but wanted to say no? If you did decline, did you feel guilty? Somehow, we become conditioned to believe that it is impolite to decline a request for help, especially when it comes from the boss.

Trying to do everything you are asked or invited to do risks stretching yourself too thin and performing below your usual level of competence. Many teachers sustain 60- or 70-hour work weeks, arriving at school early, staying late, and attending meetings. As dedicated, caring educators, we can always see more to do or more we feel we should do. To survive hectic demands, however, we must decline some opportunities. Though saying no can be difficult, answering yes to every request sets you on an accelerated path to frustration and burnout. See **Stress** and **Worry**.

As the only person who can protect you and your time, you must decide whether worrying about what someone thinks is more important than protecting yourself from being overworked and overwhelmed. Saying no can benefit your overall wellness because it helps you stay in balance.

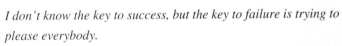

I don't know the key to success, but the key to failure is trying to please everybody.
Bill Cosby, comedian and education advocate

Declining requests

If you struggle with "no," you may find it easier to accept what others send your way than to hold your ground and protect your time. To change the tendency to respond yes, decide where your boundaries lie and which responsibilities seem reasonable to accept. Follow your intuition and wisdom, selecting activities you enjoy or need for your career and life goals. Decline requests that will cause stress, interfere with other commitments, or make you uncomfortable. Declining requests can be done with grace: explain that until you fulfill current obligations, you regret that you will be unable to help this time. Use a professional, but firm, voice to avoid being pressured.

"CAN I COUNT ON YOU TO COACH VOLLEYBALL?
IT ONLY TAKES A FEW HOURS A WEEK."

Occupational Wellness

Occupational wellness includes:

- attitude toward your career;
- contributing your talent and knowledge to work that is personally significant and satisfying;
- making career choices consistent with personal values and interests;
- job satisfaction and professional ambitions; and
- overall performance on the job.
  (National Wellness Institute 2007)

In general, occupational wellness recognizes your personal satisfaction and enrichment in life through professional activities. For some, having an occupation provides a way to use time. Without a job, people can become bored, depressed, or even destructive. An individual's occupation provides purpose for life and includes aspects of emotional, intellectual, spiritual, physical, and social wellness. Occupational health, then, comes down to finding a balance between work and leisure time, addressing workplace stress, and building relationships with co-workers. See **Balance**.

One important aspect of occupational wellness is deciding that you are in the right profession. Because work encompasses a large percentage of your time, it is important for your overall well-being to do what you love and love what you do. When you are doing what you were meant to do, your sense of meaning and purpose increase.

How is your occupational wellness on the job?

Review signs of optimal occupational wellness for teachers (Wilcock 2006):

- satisfaction with what you do with your life;
- comfort with the direction of your future within the profession;
- ability to assess accurately your strengths and weaknesses as a teacher;
- interest and enjoyment in activities associated with school;
- belief that you have the personal qualities of a valuable and valued teacher;
- excitement toward planning and implementing instruction; and
- satisfaction with a job well-done.

Optimism

Pessimists usually get what they expect. So do optimists. Believing in yourself increases your chances of success.
John Maxwell, authority on leadership

Do you perceive a partially filled glass to be half-full or half-empty? How do you usually interpret your circumstances? Do you focus on what appears to be going wrong in your environment or what is going well?

Optimism involves expectations for a positive outcome. Although everyone experiences setbacks, an optimist sees setbacks as temporary occurrences that can be overcome. Interestingly enough, people are not born as optimistic or pessimistic. In reality, the way a person views the world is influenced by his or her experiences in life. According to Seligman (2002), people trained to look at the bright side of their circumstances actually suffered fewer illnesses than their peers who did not experience the same training. He also suggested that people can harness the power of optimism into positive thinking.

In your day-to-day teaching, you will face many issues in which you must control how you think. For example, if you resent suggestions for improvement made during an observation by your principal and allow your thoughts to impose a pessimistic view of your longevity in the field, you could miss a golden opportunity to develop or refine your skills. Similarly, if you focus on the negative only, you could overlook important confidence-building praise regarding techniques you masterfully implemented. Get past feeling gloomy or angry, and strive to keep perspective with a hopeful, cheerful outlook. See **Attitude** and **Expressing Yourself in Words**.

Optimism—catch it!

You know how yawning is contagious? Well, so is optimism! Optimism breeds enthusiasm, and enthusiasm is contagious. The way to get others excited is to be excited yourself. If you view a lesson as (yawn) dull and boring, your students will experience it as such. Conversely, if you demonstrate a keen interest in the topic and a desire to share what you know, your students will be more inclined to listen and learn content. Convey optimism by adding a little life to your voice—like the tone you would use to greet a friend you haven't seen in a while. If optimism is contagious, then so is pessimism. Don't think so? Try starting any lesson by saying, "I don't think you will like this topic, but you have to know it for the test." Without a doubt, your students will either dislike the lesson or find it challenging. See **Believing in Yourself and Others**.

Organizational Skills

Being organized may or may not come naturally to you, but you can improve your organizational skills with a little effort and practice. In the end, becoming more organized will save you time and reduce anxieties.

Boost your organizational skills with these tips.

- Keep a hard copy or electronic file of materials on every topic you teach.
- Locate and organize all manipulatives and other instructional materials you need for the next day's schoolwork before going home for the day.
- Return materials each day to their storage places to avoid disorganized piles.
- Purchase inexpensive bins and storage crates for instructional supplies.
- Arrive at school early each day to get a handle on your responsibilities.
- Make a daily to-do list to remind yourself of priorities and keep you on task.
- Write frequently used directions or routines on a chart, laminate it, and post it with magnets on the chalkboard instead of rewriting the same instructions.
- Buy rubber stamps of messages you often use while grading.
- Dispose of outdated materials.
- Photograph favorite bulletin boards or displays of student work and file the photos with the appropriate unit.
- Wear a garden apron or tool belt to organize stickers, stamps, markers, scissors, glue, and other sundry supplies often needed when monitoring and working with primary students.

Passion

A teacher affects eternity; he can never tell where his influence stops.

Henry Brooks Adams, journalist, historian, and academic

Why did you become a teacher? Do you want to change the future? Do you delight in watching students learn? Does your face light up each time you mention your students? If so, keep that passion alive! The teaching profession needs you!

On the other hand, if you have lost the burning excitement you once felt, you can regenerate joy in teaching by:

- listening to the stories of inspiring teachers;
- talking through frustrations with a friend or other trusted teacher;
- contacting a former mentor for insight and advice;
- reflecting on where and when your energy goes "flat";
- playing "what if" to visualize your perfect teaching experience; and
- noticing opportunities to teach creatively, when you might teach "outside the box."

You may need to make a bigger investment to rekindle your passion. You might register for a special workshop, enroll in a class with a revered college professor, change grade-levels, or take on a new role for the school. Personal rejuvenation through a new hobby (see **Hobbies**) may renew your passion for work. We encourage you to seek passion; otherwise, your lack of enthusiasm can make you, your colleagues, and all the students and families with whom you work miserable. Unhappy teachers can crush the hopes and inspiration of their students.

It is worth mentioning that reasonable people go through peaks and valleys in their careers and that some do change careers from time to time. Desires, situations, and needs change. If you are experiencing what you consider to be serious difficulty, feel a heaviness that is difficult to explain, or dread Monday mornings on Saturday evenings, it is time to talk with someone you trust. Seek advice, explore your options, and gather your resources, but realize that only you can decide whether to stay in the job or resign to pursue a fresh professional endeavor. See **Attitude**, **Balance**, **Dropping Out**, **Joy**, **Mentoring**, and **Occupational Wellness**.

Perspective

You might be surprised to read that it isn't so much what happens in your life that causes your body to respond. Rather, it's what you think about those events that can create physical, emotional, and social problems. The pattern of distress generally occurs when a situation is perceived negatively and you mull over it, imagining all sorts of consequences. Your body then responds physiologically with increased blood pressure, heart palpitations, nausea, sweaty palms, or an upset stomach. The major downside to this thinking is that you focus your energy on your problems and bad things that could happen.

Suppose, for example, that you are about to be observed by your principal. You believe the principal ignored you in the hall last week and fear that your careless gossip has gotten back to the office. Imagining many unpleasant ways your professional life could change by being on the outs with the principal, you decide to send an e-mail to explain how hurt you are at being ignored and that you want to clear the air before your observation. Unfortunately, the principal never saw you in the hall that day and did not know about the gossip. Instead of resolving a negative situation, your action created one. Now, you are worrying about what the principal thinks of you.

To escape this stressful mind-set, you might apply cognitive restructuring or reframing. This technique has you look at a distressful situation from as many different points of view as possible, examining each to select one that seems reasonable. Reframing can help reduce your negative thoughts, feelings, and emotions (Seaward 2006).

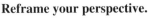

Reframe your perspective.
- Calm your mind to allow yourself to see alternative interpretations.
- Acknowledge your current interpretations and possible motivations for hanging onto them.
- Modify your expectations of yourself and others.
- Give the new interpretation a place in your emotional psyche.
- Eliminate negative self-talk by giving yourself positive affirmations.

Physical Wellness

Physical wellness includes:

- consuming health-enhancing foods;
- maintaining fitness with regular activity;
- recognizing that looking and feeling good relate to increased self-esteem, self-control, and a sense of direction;
- monitoring your vital signs;
- providing medical self-care and knowing when to seek help from a medical professional; and
- being vigilant of your alcohol, tobacco, and drug consumption. (National Wellness Institute 2007)

The physical dimension of wellness is the component of health most often recognized in Western society. Who doesn't want to look great and feel terrific? Attending to physical wellness means consuming a healthy diet, exercising, and avoiding high-risk behaviors. See **Body Image**, **Body Mass Index**, **Choices**, **Diet**, **Habits**, **Humor**, **X-ercise**, and **ZZZs.**

How is your physical wellness on the job?

Signs of optimal physical wellness for teachers include:

- having stamina to get through the work day;
- eating a healthy lunch and snacks;
- incorporating movement during instruction and free time;
- maintaining a clean classroom environment;
- dressing professionally with comfortable clothing and shoes;
- avoiding eyestrain with appropriate light and frequent breaks; and
- seeing a health care professional when symptoms of illness first appear.

Prioritizing

Keep the most immediate and important tasks at the top of your to-do list. When faced with a long list, note tasks that must be completed as soon as possible. If you have difficulty starting a huge task, break it down into smaller steps and tackle an easier piece. Completing even part of your list will generate positive feelings, motivate you to continue, and ultimately help build your confidence for the next daunting task.

Prioritizing in action

It's Sunday and you have to plan lessons for the week, grade a set of tests, plan a party that is still a few weeks away, cook dinner for your family, and return a telephone call to a friend. You might create a list in sequential order by priority that looks something like this:

- Thaw meat from freezer.
- Develop lesson plans.
- Place dinner in oven.
- Grade tests while dinner is cooking.
- Eat dinner with family.
- Call friend.
- Begin party planning.

Now prioritize the same list using the ACT Model. Use an A for items that "Absolutely must get done that day," a C for items that "Could get done," and a T for those that you will "Try to get done" (Blonna 2007).

A – Thaw meat from freezer.

A – Develop lesson plans.

A – Place dinner in oven.

A – Grade tests while dinner is cooking.

A – Eat dinner with family.

C – Call friend.

T – Begin party planning.

Quality Time

To most people, quality time means concentrated, uninterrupted time to spend with those you love. Finding that time can be a challenge! Regardless how much work you complete in your classroom each day, you always will find additional lessons to plan, papers to grade, instructional materials to create, and calls to make. Taking work home is common. Yet, night after night, weekend after weekend, it eventually can lead to resentment in significant others who want more time with you. The result can stress you and your relationships. It's worth getting creative about how you carve out quality time.

Protect quality time with loved ones.
- Complete paperwork during planning time when possible.
- Arrive early each Monday, before the office gets busy, to use the copier and set up the week's instructional materials. Alternately, stay late each Friday to prepare materials for the upcoming week.
- Limit the hours or number of days you stay late and stick to that schedule.
- Review assignments to determine other ways to evaluate student performance. Some assignments require little time for students to complete, but take a long time to grade.
- Delegate appropriate classroom tasks to volunteers. See **Volunteer for a Win-Win Way to Well-Being**.

Okay, you followed these suggestions, but an extracurricular position has cut into your after-school time. If you must work at home:
- talk honestly with your loved ones about why you need to do school work during your time together; and
- agree that you will not substitute your work responsibilities for agreed-upon family activities—dinnertime, game night, important projects, or helping with homework.

Spend quality time with students, too.
Create unique opportunities for quality time with your students. Identify, plan, and devote instructional time to lessons that create good experiences for you and the class. Encourage your students to relax, enjoy, and accept one another. You might set up a modern version of show-and-tell during which students share their thoughts, feelings, and experiences with their classmates within a given structure or fun activity.

Quiet Time

You work in a noisy environment: the busy hum of students completing their work; the grinding of the pencil sharpener and swishing of papers pulled from desks; the clicking classroom heater, buzzing fluorescent lights, and whirring computers; school bells ringing, and intercom announcements blaring. On some days, these sounds blend into white noise; other days, those noises may subtly ease into your consciousness, disturbing your concentration and irritating your last nerve.

On noisy days, find quiet time! Create moments to breathe, relax, stretch, take a walk, or meditate. Though it may seem luxurious, remember that busy people can burn out (see **Stress**). At the end of the day, take time to renew your mind before you begin your next round of responsibilities.

Close your eyes and rest. Reflect on your day, examine your feelings, and consider the underlying thoughts that guided your actions . . . or think about nothing. Sit on a park bench or stretch out on your bed. Pray or complete another spiritual activity such as meditating. Whatever you decide to do or not do, spend this time alone. Even 10 minutes can rejuvenate you. Also see **Breathing Techniques**, **Relaxation**, and **Spiritual Wellness**.

Rejuvenate at school.
- Take an afternoon stretch with students.
- Enjoy a cup of your favorite herbal tea while planning lessons.
- Change the wallpaper on your computer's desktop.
- Listen to your favorite music.

Quiet time doesn't have to be still.
Strap on your helmet and go motorcycle riding, attend dance class, go fishing, work in your garden, sing with the choir, play a sport, visit a spa, or sky-dive. Movement can fill your quiet time, as long as it rejuvenates you and takes you away from your daily grind. It's all about quieting your spirit and staying in balance. Also see **Balance** and **Hobbies**.

Reflection

Reflection is a way to attain self-awareness. According to Goleman (1995), self-awareness is the most crucial source of emotional intelligence. The reflective process requires you to step back from your busy life to examine your thinking, feelings, and explanatory style. Examine your moods, strengths, and needs as they arise, without getting caught up in the emotions surrounding them.

Begin reflecting by answering a few questions: How was your day? Did instruction go the way you planned? Did student behavior align with your rules and procedures? Are you pleased with the way you mentored your teacher intern? Did you exercise this morning? How healthy was your food intake? What changes would you make to improve? Asking yourself questions about your work, activities, feelings, and other experiences is a reflective tool for self-examination and a stimulus for behavior change. Being a reflective practitioner is one way to attend to your occupational wellness because it helps you recognize strengths, identify goals, and note progress.

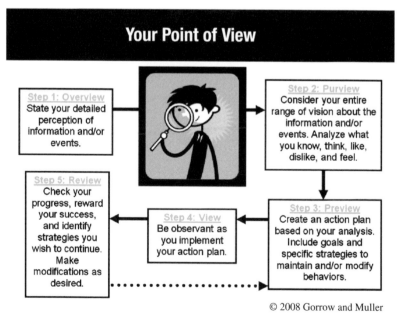

© 2008 Gorrow and Muller

Relaxation

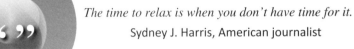

The time to relax is when you don't have time for it.
Sydney J. Harris, American journalist

Teachers tend to be service-oriented, often extending themselves for many things and for many people—sometimes to their own detriment. Are you stretched too thin? Remember that superheroes exist in the movies and comic books, not in your house or classroom (even if you do have a cape). When you push too hard, your body signals you with headaches, an upset stomach, fatigue, anxiety, insomnia, or irritability. It's probably trying to warn you to slow down. You need rest and freedom from responsibilities. So, on your to-do list, be sure to list relax—and do it each day. No guilt, just ah-h-h-h!

How? Relaxation involves loosening up or letting go. By lessening control or pressure, you can restore energy that has been used during your daily activities. With discretion, relaxation techniques can be practiced anywhere or anytime, because they can be as simple as breathing slowly and practicing focused muscle relaxation (Romas and Sharma 2007). Just find a method that works for you. See related information in **No's Aren't Always Negative** and **Quiet Time**.

Ah-h-h-h! Practice relaxation now.
- Close your eyes and take three deep breaths in through your nose, exhaling slowly out of your mouth. Now picture yourself at the beach. Feel the warm sand hugging your toes and sense the brilliant rays of the sun engulfing your body, absorbing your tension. Hear the chatter of seagulls flying overhead and the steady rhythm of breaking waves lapping against the shore. Let those waves carry you out onto the ocean. Safely you are drifting afloat in the wide sea, calm and peaceful. Let its serenity surround you. Ah-h-h-h!

- Close your eyes to take a virtual walk in the woods. Imagine a crisp autumn day and feel the cool breeze gently brushing your face and hair. Picture the vibrant and sun-drenched hues of golden, crimson, and orange leaves, some drifting downward as they exit their branches preparing for winter's entrance. Hear fallen leaves crunch and crackle beneath your feet as you meander a sheltered path through the quiet woods, letting your concerns fade away, like the wispy smoke of a distant campfire. Quiet and calm fill you. Ah-h-h-h!

EVEN SUPERHEROES NEED DOWN TIME

Rewarding Yourself

You made it an entire week without being late to school! You're trying to quit smoking and you managed all day without a cigarette! You earned tenure! A student who has not spoken all year in class asked you a question! Whatever the goal, you see progress. Celebrate success. Reward yourself!

We generally tend to repeat rewarded behaviors and discard those that are not rewarded. Therefore, if you are working to break a bad habit and see progress toward that goal, systematically rewarding yourself for good behavior will strengthen your ability to perform that behavior. Of course, the reward should not negate the positive outcome of your new behavior. Don't reward not smoking all week with a cigarette.

"Yay for me!"

- Reward even small accomplishments with something you value (don't punish your goofs).
- Match your reward with the effort (playing a round of golf on your favorite course or buying a new outfit for losing 5 pounds is more helpful in the big picture than splurging on a hot fudge sundae).
- Tell others about your success (yes, Virginia, it is okay to brag, but avoid rubbing your success in the face of someone struggling with your same issue).
- Make lemonade if things go sour. Look for the good in a bad outcome and make a new plan.
- Design a behavior-plan contract. Outline changes you desire and identify potential rewards at incremental levels.
- Evaluate your progress, goals, and rewards—it is okay to make changes.
- Reduce rewards over time and let the new behaviors become your standard.

What behavior do you want to change? _____

_____

What rewards will encourage your motivation to change? _____

_____

What rewards might defeat your effort toward change? _____

_____

Safety

Attend to your personal safety and the safety of others by behaving in ways that reduce the risk of injury or illness. Personal safety includes buckling your seat belt and wearing sunscreen. But what about promoting safety at school? You might consider these keys:

- Practice several ways to contact the office in case of an emergency.
- Know all possible school entrances and exits.
- Avoid leaving school doors propped open during recess.
- Be aware of special circumstances regarding custodial rights of your students.
- Review permanent record folders for each student to determine allergies and other special needs.
- Take your cell phone when you report for duties or supervise recess.
- Open your classroom door while meeting with students or parents/ guardians, particularly if your door does not have a window.
- Take the class roster with you on emergency practice drills and call roll each time.
- Ask an administrator or team teacher to attend parent/guardian conferences you must schedule after the school day.
- Avoid working alone in your classroom during evening hours.
- Park in a well-lit area.

Social Wellness

Social wellness includes:

- living in harmony with other people and your environment;
- preserving nature;
- recognizing the impact you have on your environment;
- developing friendships;
- improving personal relationships;
- living in harmony instead of conflict;
- thinking of others; and
- contributing to your community.
  (National Wellness Institute 2007)

In general, social wellness includes striving to get along peacefully with others, enhancing relationships, and actively participating in community events. Because spending quality time with the people you love is an important part of staying in balance, plan downtime with family and friends so that you can relax and have fun. Also look for opportunities to enjoy colleagues inside and outside of the school environment. The power to build rapport and connect with your environment rests with you. Avoid missing out on important social networks because you are too focused on occupational and intellectual wellness. See **Balance** and **Hobbies**.

How is your wellness on the job?

Signs of optimal social wellness for teachers include:

- establishing positive student-teacher-parent/guardian relationships;
- teaching students to work cooperatively with others;
- building rapport with colleagues and developing trusting relationships with mentors;
- actively participating in school events;
- contributing to school-level decision-making by committee work and other service;
- organizing school activities that benefit the community; and
- networking with other teachers through professional development activities.

Savvy social strategies

- Have a dessert party in your classroom for all faculty and staff—each person must bring a dessert to attend.
- Plan a potluck dinner with each course served in a different home or classroom.
- Organize a shopping trip to an outlet center and wear school-spirit clothing.
- Arrange a tailgate party before a sports event.
- Join, as a grade-level team, a club around your favorite hobby.
- Organize a fund-raiser for a local charity.

The i in illness is isolation, and the crucial letters in wellness are we.

Author unknown, as quoted by Mimi Guarneri in *The Heart Speaks: A Cardiologist Reveals the Secret Language of Healing*

Connect with colleagues.

The typical teacher works primarily in isolation from other adults. According to Henderson and Milstein (2003), restructuring your work day so that you have opportunities to interact meaningfully with your colleagues can increase your chances of remaining in the teaching profession. Undeniably, this strategy made a difference for Jenna, a teacher assigned some of the most at-risk students in her grade level. Simply overwhelmed that first month of school, Jenna wondered whether teaching was really for her. Doubting whether she was doing anything the "right" way, she invited her assigned mentor to observe her and asked to observe her mentor. Jenna wanted feedback from a teacher prior to a formal observation by her administrators, and she anticipated observing the way her mentor handled transitions and routines.

As a result of those observations, Jenna realized that she was right on target—she just needed experience to gain confidence. To show her appreciation, Jenna invited her mentor to dinner where they engaged in school-talk for hours. They decided to plan together, as well as co-teach a lesson in an upcoming unit. They also realized that they enjoyed similar hobbies. Jenna's mentor paved the way into professional opportunities and shared social connections that proved invaluable. More than 25 years following their first meeting, their friendship is still strong. Jenna attributes much of her early success to the collegial relationship and has admitted many times that her career would have suffered greatly had it not been for this treasured colleague and friend.

Space at School

Could a person get lost in your classroom? Do you have lots of stuff and a poorly organized seating arrangement for students? According to Girdano et al. (2005), when people are forced to share space under conditions they perceive as crowded, stress levels rise and behavior can be influenced negatively. Maybe it's time to review your classroom setup.

"I CAN'T UNDERSTAND WHY I'M FEELING SO TENSE AND STRESSED."

- Look at the physical arrangement of your classroom.
- Arrange students' desks and chairs so that everyone can comfortably view the board or screen.
- Consider personal space needs and maximize traffic flow patterns.
- Allow space for cooperative learning groups, as well as individual work opportunities.
- Assign small-group activities away from individual desks.
- Discard outdated materials and displays to increase space.

Spiritual Wellness

Spiritual wellness includes:

- the search for purpose and meaning in life;
- appreciating the depth of life and natural forces in the universe;
- finding harmony between personal emotions and life's journey; and
- experiencing living a life consistent with values and beliefs. (National Wellness Institute 2007)

Spirituality is generally based on your perceptions of a power that is greater than you, part of a larger whole, and beyond what can be explained in the natural. It exists in every aspect of life, providing purpose, meaning, guidance, and a source of strength to help one persevere along life's journey (Karren et al. 2006). Spiritual beliefs help you establish values, a code of ethics, bonding opportunities with others, empathy, compassion, and humanitarianism. Difficult times are easier to weather if you strive to stay in balance (see **Balance**) and regularly attend to your spirituality. Here are ways to attend to your spirituality.

- Reflect on your values and beliefs (see **Reflection**).
- Examine your view of the spiritual realm, the unifying power that cannot be explained in the natural.
- Pray.
- Worship alone and with others who believe as you do.
- Evaluate relationships for harmony and meaning (see **Social Wellness**).
- Determine your life purpose.
- Check harmony with self (see **Acceptance**).

Spirituality is not a one-time happening as much as a process: self-reflect, pray, check for harmony, and repeat. Set aside time to make adjustments. By the way, did you assess your Spiritual Wellness? See **Extras**.

How is your wellness on the job?

Signs of optimal spiritual wellness for teachers include:

- feeling satisfied that the teaching profession provides purpose for your life;
- maintaining harmonious and meaningful relationships with school stakeholders;
- having your values and beliefs in sync with your teaching responsibilities;
- taking time to reflect upon your work;
- using effective breathing techniques;
- capturing quiet moments in your school day to relax, stretch, walk, or meditate; and
- keeping things in perspective.

Stress

Being in control of your life and having realistic expectations about your day-to-day challenges are the keys to stress management, which is perhaps the most important ingredient to living a happy, healthy and rewarding life.

Marilu Henner, American actress

Studies on stress in the workplace have demonstrated a link between job stress and unhealthy behaviors, such as overindulging in alcohol and poor eating habits, and increased rates of heart disease and other illnesses (Bryner 2006). Signs of stress can include:

- feeling more critical or sarcastic at work;
- lacking job satisfaction and joy;
- experiencing difficulty getting started on work-related tasks;
- showing less patience or more irritability toward others at work; and
- lacking energy to be productive.

Furthermore, stress, including school- and job-related pressures and family concerns, is named as the top reason for sleeping difficulties (National Sleep Foundation 2007). While some people believe that they work best under stressful conditions, the potential long-term harm outweighs any short-term benefits. Even rubber bands snap when stretched too thin.

As most of us know, the demands of teaching are great and occupational dimension of our lives can affect the other dimensions (see **Balance**). According to Culbert (2006), though some stress appears to invigorate and boost ability to focus, too much stress actually decreases efficiency, eventually negatively affecting one's health. She outlined Herbert Benson's steps to optimize performance from his book *The Breakout Principle* (2003), as follows.

- Struggle: Focus on your problem to experience peak stress until you stop feeling productive.
- Walk Away: Do something that causes you to relax and experience a physiological change.

- Be Open: Feel relaxed while immersed in work so that performance seems automatic.
- Return to Normal: Some stress is good, but recognize when it becomes unproductive and disrupt those times with relaxation activities.

Consider talking with a trusted health professional, your mentor, or school guidance counselor for support in managing your stress levels. Pay attention to what your body is telling you, take care of yourself, and strive to stay in balance to best attend to your overall wellness. Ignoring symptoms of unproductive stress is harmful to your body, emotions, and relationships.

What does teacher burnout look like?

Composed primarily of three dimensions, (emotional exhaustion, depersonalization, and reduced personal accomplishment), burnout was a term originally used to describe healthcare workers who were physically and psychologically depleted, but has been expanded to include teachers (Vandenberghe and Huberman 1999).

How do you know whether you are burning out? In general, teachers experiencing burnout show signs of emotional exhaustion and feel unable to give as much of themselves to their students as they once did. As burnout progresses, the teacher becomes more cynical; feels more detached from students, parents and colleagues; demonstrates less empathy for students; is less tolerant of classroom disruptions; is less prepared for class each day; and exhibits a reduced commitment to the profession.

What causes burnout? Role ambiguity, where a teacher is unclear about responsibilities or goals, can generate occupational stress and increase the likelihood of burnout. The cure? Expectations and available support must be clarified by administrators, and teachers need to ask questions. Another common stressor is student misbehavior. Chronic behavior problems that lack clear resolution particularly can lead to teacher burnout.

Time for Wellness

Taking time for your health is really what this handy alpha guide on wellness is all about. You have an exercise routine, but you don't have time for it. You know you should spend more time with your friends, but everyone is too busy to get together. Your colleague is going on a European vacation and you cannot even remember your last vacation. What is a vacation anyway?

Now might be the time to hit the pause button in your mind. Think about how much time you typically spend attending to each dimension of wellness. Review your self-assessment or take it again (see **Extras**). Life changes! It is helpful to check your wellness periodically to help yourself keep balanced.

How balanced are your dimensions of wellness?

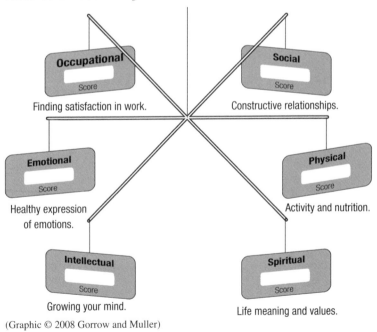

(Graphic © 2008 Gorrow and Muller)

How are the arms of your mobile? Do one or two dip greatly or elevate far above the others? It may be time to review **Balance** and specific dimensions of wellness and make the most of your time!

Time Management

There are 1,440 minutes each day. You might be one of those people who continually says, "I wish I had more time." Nevertheless, everyone gets the same amount of time in each 24-hour period. You can't save it for another day, so how you use your time speaks volumes about you.

> *When you give someone your time, you are giving them a portion of your life that you'll never get back. Your time is your life. That is why the greatest gift you can give someone is your time.*
> Rick Warren, minister and author

Time management for effective instruction

- Use one calendar to schedule all classes, special activities, conferences, and meetings.
- Prepare and have all required instructional materials ready at the beginning of each lesson.
- Begin class promptly.
- State expected learning outcomes and provide brief transitions between activities.
- Pace instruction with a balance of direct, guided, and independent learning opportunities.
- Use an overhead timer (an electronic timer that projects onto a screen) during cooperative learning activities to help students observe and take responsibility for time.
- Allow time at the end of each lesson for summarizing, revisiting outcomes, and answering questions.
- Balance the need to watch the clock with the individual learning needs of your students.
- Engage students proficiently to increase their achievement:
  o Allocate most of the instructional time assigned to that subject or period to the student outcomes agreed upon in your curriculum—avoid tangents.
  o Keep explanations to a minimum—30 seconds to two minutes is a good range for introducing a topic and arousing interest.

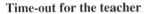

Time-out for the teacher

Your negotiated teaching contract most likely includes at least two personal days in addition to your sick leave. Consider taking a time-out for you! Complete the official paperwork in advance and plan a special wellness day for yourself at least once every school year. Do what you love, or do nothing at all, but make it an all-about-you-day without any guilt. Now, if you are a teacher who strives for perfect attendance and has not taken a day off in 15 years, this suggestion might not work for you. The guilt of missing a day, the worry that students may not have sound instruction, or the disappointment in breaking your perfect attendance record could spoil the intent of having time to yourself. Like every other tip in this book, we recommend that you make decisions based on your personal beliefs and values.

Using Your Resources

List all of the stakeholders connected to your school, including parents, guardians, community members, businesses, and nonprofit organizations. Who else do you know? Remember that other people can serve as resources for you. Also, keep track of your favorite Internet links, school and teacher supply catalogs, and bookstores. As soon as you have a need, consider the most reasonable place to seek help instead of relying on yourself for everything. Planning a unit? Collaborate and co-teach with your colleagues. Not sure how to reach a student having behavior problems? Communicate with the school counselor or special needs educator. Need another pair of hands? Ask for classroom volunteers. Why go it alone? Together, we are stronger than any of us are as individuals.

Variety

THE BORED OF EDUCATION

Sure, variety is the spice of life, but how about at school? Without variety in your lesson plans, your instruction will become routine and dull. If you need help, check into the many great resources available on multiple intelligences, learning styles, and cooperative learning (see **Resources** in the **Extras** section). Incorporating new techniques and different styles of instructional modes keeps delivery fresh and increases the potential of addressing the diverse learning needs of your students. You'll feel rejuvenated when your students notice how creatively you are working for their benefit and you see their curiosity bloom.

Learning happens in various situations, even when students wait in line. Seize those moments! Having a variety of fillers to use during such moments encourages spontaneity in teaching and learning!
Cynthia Curran, Division Director, Teaching and Learning Support, DOE, Alaska

Visualization

If one advances confidently in the direction of his dreams, and endeavors to live the life which he has imagined, he will meet with success unexpected in common hours.
Henry David Thoreau, American author

It's been said that you are what you eat, but have you considered that you can be what you see in your mind's eye? Let's say that you've been asked to demonstrate a teaching strategy during an upcoming faculty meeting. The principal happened to visit your class when you were using this particular technique and suggested that your peers would enjoy learning how to present the activity. Before you could decline, your name was added to the meeting agenda. Though you are very comfortable presenting to your students, you feel extremely nervous when you must speak in front of your peers. What can you do to prepare? Try visualization, a strategy in which you picture yourself performing the desired behavior. To practice visualization:

- define your desired goal;
- relax your body and your mind;
- tell yourself "I can do this.";
- envision every little detail of the event including the finer points, such as the place and people around you, what you are doing, and how you are feeling; and
- practice this routine regularly until you are comfortable seeing yourself completing the task.

Visualizing success

In this example, your goal is to demonstrate effectively a teaching strategy during a faculty meeting.

- Relax. Tell yourself, "I know this strategy inside and out. My kids love it! It would be great to share it with other teachers. I can do this." Then, in your mind's eye, imagine your colleagues as students, or whatever other image helps you gain perspective and reduces your anxiety.
- Visualize the meeting room—complete with the table displaying manipulatives and other materials. See the faces of your colleagues, think through each step you will demonstrate, and feel yourself gradually relaxing and enjoying the opportunity.
- Close your eyes and visualize the successful completion of your presentation.
- Repeat the visualization daily until it is time to present.
- Be thoroughly prepared by organizing all materials in advance.

Volunteering—
a Win-Win Way to Well-Being

As a teacher, you are one of the busiest people on the planet.
Nonetheless, consider volunteering for a worthwhile cause to enhance
your own well-being. Along with helping others, volunteering
increases your feelings of self-worth and improves your health.
According to authors Insel and Roth (2008), volunteers report several
benefits including feeling more calm and relaxed, having a perception
of better health, catching fewer colds, feeling relief from chronic pains
associated with arthritis, and experiencing fewer asthmatic episodes.

It is not just about room mothers—recruit classroom volunteers.
We've established that you are a very busy person! Of course, you
can hire help in your personal life, but what about your classroom?
How can others help out? In the old days, we eagerly sought room
mothers to bake goodies, chaperone field trips, and help with parties
and end-of-the-year activities. We've come a long way, colleagues!
Yes, recruit parents and guardians, but also look for others,
including community members and retired teachers, to assist with
those everyday responsibilities that leave you longing for an extra
set of hands. Be sure to clear all volunteers through your office
according to the school district policy and provide a brief training
session for them.

Volunteers can help you:

- tutor students having difficulties;
- work with a cooperative group during an instructional activity;
- read to students;
- help students who were absent to fill in the gaps and get caught up
  on assignments;
- copy papers, laminate, or make learning activities;
- grade objective assignments (Grade subjective work yourself and
  keep grades confidential.);
- find resources in the community for special classroom projects; and
- search the Internet and other resources for instructional information
  you seek.

Students make great classroom helpers, too. Involve them in returning items to appropriate storage, maintaining the classroom, decorating bulletin boards, and setting up the room for the next day. You don't have to do everything. Really!

Walking for Wellness

Walking can improve health, prevent heart disease, and maintain body weight. It is a convenient activity that does not require special equipment or clothing and is considered safer than vigorous exercise. Walking is a great and easy way to incorporate aerobic exercise, which is recommended for weight control, into your daily routine. On a walk you can take in fresh air, enjoy landscapes, and attend to your spiritual wellness.

Begin a daily walking program with stretching and a slow-paced walk, gradually progressing to a more rapid pace. Increasing your speed or the amount of time that you walk boosts the effectiveness of your program (Howley and Franks 2007). The American College of Sports Medicine and the American Heart Association (2007) concur that walking is a great form of exercise of moderately intense physical activity. These organizations recommend that healthy adults under age 65 walk a minimum of 30 minutes, five days a week, moving briskly enough to sweat and increase heart rate, yet carry on a conversation.

Work in walking daily.
- Plan a walking field trip with your students.
- Walk with other teachers in your grade-level team during lunch to plan projects and develop relationships.
- Walk around the playground when on recess duty rather than stand in one place.
- Plan with the physical education teacher a school-wide walk-a-thon for a special fund-raiser or health event.
- Walk your pet before and after school.

Worry

"STOP, THIEF!"

Dyer (1976) defined worry as the immobilization of thinking in the present moment as a result of the preoccupation with things that may, or may not, occur in the future. Worry is characterized by feeling anxious, distressed, or troubled. Though worry may be seen as an act of compassion for others, it is a waste of your time. It makes you focus on things that could go wrong rather than on possible positive outcomes or creative problem-solving solutions. Most of all, worry steals your joy, robs you of hope, and destroys your peace. When the worry wheels begin to spin, disengage them: reframe your thinking, purposely choose to do an activity you love (see **Hobbies** and **Joy**). Quit worrying and spend your time in a proactive, healthy mode for your overall well-being.

Are you a worry-wart?

Signs of too much worry, according to Shearer and Gordon (2006), include:

- being uncomfortable with uncertainty;
- having an upset stomach or irritable bowel;
- exhibiting feelings of self-doubt and/or excessive pessimism;
- experiencing an inability to concentrate or sleep; and
- having chronic anxiety.

Reduce worry—weed out trivia.

Do you obsess about details or think that if you don't step in, the job will not get done? Are those little things causing you anxiousness? It may be time to take a step back. Distinguish between what needs attention and what needs *your* attention. Avoid getting bogged down in minor problems and micromanaging every detail. Let students help make decisions and share responsibilities in the classroom. Don't try to "do it all, all the time."

X-ercise

Exercise is essential for your health. It helps improve your level of fitness, maintain a desirable body weight, moderate your moods, and provide opportunities for social interactions. It can be a powerful way to lift your spirits and enhance your overall outlook on life. Before starting an exercise program, it is important to seek the advice of a healthcare professional. However, in general, 20–30 minutes of daily aerobic exercise that increases your heart rate and incorporates rhythmic movement of large muscle groups (chest, back, arms, legs, and buttocks) is recommended by the American College of Sports Medicine (Wygand and Cahill 2006).

Pick up the pace.

- Provide opportunities for movement during instruction.
- Monitor on your feet instead of your seat during classroom instruction.
- Increase kinesthetic opportunities with cooperative learning and other collaborative teaching strategies.
- Take breaks from paperwork to walk or stretch during your planning period.
- Park away from the school building to allow for a comfortable walk with the materials you must carry.
- Walk to the restroom farthest away from your classroom.

100-calorie burns*
- Dancing—20 minutes at a moderate pace
- Gardening—15 minutes of digging or raking
- Housework—25 minutes of vigorous housework
- Walking—15 minutes of brisk walking

*Based on a 150-pound individual (Calzadilla 2008)

X-tra Pay for X-tra Duty

Teachers take on many responsibilities beyond regular classroom instruction, often as volunteers. Ask your principal whether the leadership opportunity you have been asked to accept tenders a stipend. Many extracurricular activities give stipends, including yearbook and other club advising, as well as coaching and teacher-in-charge duties. A little extra cash for extra effort sure helps ease financial burdens or add to classroom resources, and enhances your occupational wellness.

Your Words Are Powerful

Don't underestimate the power of your words. Even one-syllable utterances carry positive and negative consequences. Words can set you on a course, frame your plans, and determine your destiny. These tips can improve the quality and clarity of your speech:
- Think before you speak to determine the appropriateness of your words.
- Avoid uttering offensive remarks, even in jest; offhand comments aren't always funny or appreciated by others.
- Speak positively of your life, career, future, and family members.
- Don't complain—it makes you feel worse and gives power to a negative situation.

- Talk directly to individuals with whom you have a concern instead of talking about them to others.
- Be proactive, precise, and direct to decrease the chance of being misinterpreted or misunderstood.
- Improve your vocabulary to increase your chances of communicating clearly and accurately.
- Use audience-appropriate words.

See **Acceptance**, **Attitude**, **Believing in Yourself and Others**, **Expressing Yourself in Words**, and **Optimism**.

Zero Tolerance for Substance Abuse

You've heard the sad stories and witnessed lives torn apart by substance abuse. To reduce drinking and driving, many states have enacted zero-tolerance laws, and many school systems endorse zero-tolerance policies for substance-free environments. Hence, a word to the wise: Avoid flirting with any area of dangerous, addictive behaviors that can lead to a path of trouble in your life, or in the lives of your students. Smoking in your car during a planning period, taking drugs in a drug-free school zone, or camouflaging vodka in your soda bottle are inappropriate behaviors at work and behaviors you cannot hide over the long-term. Violating any school policies can result in being fired and your teaching certificate revoked, especially if substance abuse is involved. Aside from disrupting your physical wellness and posing a danger to yourself and others, when your senses are impaired, you may be incapable of acting responsibly on duty and could be found negligent in a court of law.

People do not always know when they are entering a danger zone with substances such as drugs and alcohol. Addictive habits can start innocently as chronic pain or stress nag at a person's resistance. Any behavior or thought pattern that disrupts your balance or violates public laws creates a reason for concern. If you long for or imbibe addictive substances while you are at work, you need to seek help. Your school guidance counselor has helpful contact information for your specific need and you might also contact your primary care physician or other health professional for referral to an appropriate agency. See **Occupational Wellness** and **Physical Wellness**.

Zest

It's not about soap—it's about experiencing life to the fullest! Take sheer delight in being alive and model this passion for life to your students. Enjoy what you have and make the best of all you have going for you. It is a waste of time to compare yourself to others, long for your good old days, dream of retirement, or approach your work with indifference because your feelings were once hurt. The result of that kind of thinking and apathy is misery. Instead, go for the gusto! LIVE!

As the popular song goes, "Don't worry, be happy!" Abraham Lincoln has been quoted as saying, "Most folks are as happy as they make up their minds to be." Have you made up your mind? Such decisions already have directly affected your overall wellness, but it is never too late to make a fresh, exciting start. We hope that you will decide to enthusiastically embrace your life. See **Attitude**, **Joy**, and **Passion**.

Zzzs

Do you need sleep? Although sleep needs vary, most adults require six to eight hours of sleep each night to function well. Lack of sleep can lead to impaired performance involving memory, logical reasoning, and learning; decreased productivity; increased perceptions of stress; and a greater need for healthcare services. It also is a contributing factor in traffic accidents and absenteeism. Stress, including school- and job-related pressures and family concerns, is named as the top reason for sleeping difficulties (National Sleep Foundation 2007).

Sleep aids without side effects

Worrying about tomorrow's schedule, reliving a difficult day, arguing before bedtime, or overindulging in bad habits interfere with a good night's rest. If sleep eludes you, try the following ideas.

- Resolve conflicts before leaving school each day.
- Maintain a regular sleep schedule—go to bed and wake at the same time each day.

- Don't go to bed angry with your spouse or other family members.
- Cut off consumption of caffeine, nicotine, and other stimulants several hours before bedtime.
- Perform relaxing activities to calm you before bedtime, like reading, meditating, or listening to music.
- Reserve your bedroom primarily for sleeping.
- Note concerns and potential solutions (write them out if necessary) before you go to bed to get them out of your system. Decide to deal with them tomorrow, because anxiety stimulates the sympathetic nervous system and makes you alert.

Make it a practice to regularly reflect on the physical, emotional, intellectual, spiritual, social, and occupational dimensions of your wellness. Take our Wellness Self-Assessment (see **Extras**) from time to time to assess your balance, and then make necessary changes to fully experience the tapestry of your life. Strive to stay in balance, be happy, and be well!

My life has been a tapestry of rich and royal hue
An everlasting vision of the ever-changing view
A wondrous, woven magic in bits of blue and gold
A tapestry to feel and see, impossible to hold.
Carole King, musician
From *Tapestry, 1971*

Extras

Balance vs. Imbalance within the Dimensions of Wellness

Indicators of Balance	Dimension of Wellness	Indicators of Imbalance
Maintain emotional control and stability Aware of emotional fluctuations Generally optimistic outlook Channel emotions in acceptable ways	Emotional	Loss of emotional control and stability Out of touch with emotional fluctuations Generally pessimistic outlook Channel emotions in inappropriate ways
Maintain clarity of thoughts Able to organize thoughts Able to process information Good verbal communication skills Acceptable written communication skills Aware of other peoples' emotions	Intellectual	Unable to maintain clarity of thoughts Disorganized thoughts Unable to process information Poor verbal communication skills Poor written communication skills Unaware of other peoples' emotions
Energetic about work-related tasks Feeling stimulated Desire to be productive Feeling of financial security	Occupational	Lack energy for work-related tasks Feeling un-stimulated No desire to be productive Feeling of financial insecurity
Feeling of overall good health Overall feeling of physical fitness High levels of muscular strength Good flexibility of joints/range of motion Good muscular/cardiovascular endurance	Physical	Signs or symptoms of physical problems Feeling physically unfit Poor levels of muscular strength Poor flexibility of joints/range of motion Poor muscular/cardiovascular endurance
Strong social network Strong interpersonal relationships Contentment with personal interactions Maintain satisfying intimate relationships	Social	Weak social network Unsatisfying interpersonal relationships Discontentment with personal interactions Unable to maintain satisfying intimate relationships
Sense of purpose in life Satisfied with sense of order in world Optimistic about future Believe that your life has meaning	Spiritual	Lack sense of purpose in life Unsure about sense of order in world Pessimistic about future Believe that your life lacks meaning

Wellness Self-Assessment Tools

How Do You Rate Your Emotional Wellness?

Rate each item using the following scale:

5 = Strongly Agree   4 = Agree   3 = Undecided   2 = Disagree   1 = Strongly Disagree

1. I am able to express my anger without exacerbating the situation.	
2. I am able to shut off feelings of worry and focus on the task at hand.	
3. I am able to express my feelings of love in socially appropriate ways.	
4. I allow myself to cry, if the situation calls for tears, without feeling shame.	
5. I am able to laugh and express joy when I feel happy.	
6. When hurt, I am able to express my feelings to the person who hurt me.	
7. I am able to acknowledge my feelings of guilt.	
8. I am comfortable acknowledging my fears.	
9. My demonstrations of affection are socially appropriate.	
10. My overall emotional disposition is fairly stable from day to day.	
Total =	

How Do You Rate Your Intellectual Wellness?

Rate each item using the following scale:

5 = Strongly Agree   4 = Agree   3 = Undecided   2 = Disagree   1 = Strongly Disagree

1. I am able to think and learn from past experiences.	
2. I am able to use critical thinking skills to analyze situations.	
3. I am curious and enjoy learning new information.	
4. I am open to new ideas, trying new activities, and learning new skills.	
5. I am not hesitant to question the standard ways of thinking or behaving.	
6. I am aware of the various factors influencing my thinking.	
7. I attempt to find creative solutions to problems.	
8. I am open to examining different ways of thinking about issues.	
9. I am able to apply the theoretical concepts that I have learned to my life.	
10. I show respect for and curiosity about those who are different from me.	
Total =	

How Do You Rate Your Occupational Wellness?

Rate each item using the following scale:

5 = Strongly Agree   4 = Agree   3 = Undecided   2 = Disagree   1 = Strongly Disagree

1. I find personal satisfaction in being a teacher.	
2. Teaching enriches my life.	
3. I maintain a positive attitude about teaching as my career.	
4. Teaching provides an avenue where I can contribute my unique talents for the benefit of my students.	
5. I find teaching to be very rewarding.	
6. Teaching brings meaning to my life.	
7. I find professional satisfaction in being a teacher.	
8. My career ambitions and aspirations are aligned with being a teacher.	
9. Selecting a career in teaching is consistent with my personal values and beliefs.	
10. My teaching career satisfies my need to be actively and productively involved.	
Total =	

How Do You Rate Your Physical Wellness?

Rate each item using the following scale:

5 = Strongly Agree   4 = Agree   3 = Undecided   2 = Disagree   1 = Strongly Disagree

1. I avoid the excessive intake of alcohol.	
2. I limit my consumption of substances that do not promote my health.	
3. My daily activities include some form of moderate exercise.	
4. I drink plenty of fluids.	
5. I read nutrition labels when selecting new products or brands of food.	
6. I feel generally vigorous and physically fit.	
7. I incorporate variety into my food selections.	
8. My hobbies include activities that promote my health.	
9. I perform activities that help me maintain adequate physical strength.	
10. I make sure to get adequate amounts of sleep.	
Total =	

How Do You Rate Your Social Wellness?

Rate each item using the following scale:

5 = Strongly Agree   4 = Agree   3 = Undecided   2 = Disagree   1 = Strongly Disagree

1. I am truthful in my communications with others.	
2. I speak in a direct manner (get to the point very quickly).	
3. I use appropriate vocabulary for my target audience.	
4. I make sure that my body language is conveying the message I intend to send.	
5. My gestures match my intended message.	
6. The tone of my voice is appropriate and matches my message.	
7. I avoid using curse words.	
8. I avoid the use of derogatory or hurtful language.	
9. I listen closely when someone is talking to me.	
10. When communicating, I am attuned to the reactions of others.	
Total =	

How Do You Rate Your Spiritual Wellness?

Rate each item using the following scale:

5 = Strongly Agree   4 = Agree   3 = Undecided   2 = Disagree   1 = Strongly Disagree

1. I sense harmony with myself, others, and some higher power.	
2. I am satisfied with the level of my faith.	
3. I am comfortable with my personal value system.	
4. I believe I have a satisfying purpose for my life.	
5. My emotions, thoughts, and relationships are in harmony.	
6. I sense that the parts of my life fit together and make sense to me.	
7. The meaning of life is evident in the world around me.	
8. My relationships provide direction and purpose to my life.	
9. My personal existence is meaningful.	
10. I sense that the various parts of life fit together in a unified pattern.	
Total =	

To interpret your scores:

1) Each Wellness Dimension Assessment has a possible score of 50. Scores between:

- **40 and 50** suggest that you perceive this particular dimension of wellness to be one for which you take responsibility and maintain a high level of wellness.
- **30 and 39** suggest that you perceive this particular dimension of wellness to be one in which you are sometimes uncertain regarding your sense of responsibility for achieving a high level of wellness.
- **10 and 29** suggest that you perceive this particular dimension of wellness to be one in which you lack a sense of responsibility for achieving a high level of wellness.
- **1 and 9** suggest that you perceive this particular dimension of wellness to be one in which you experience difficulty attaining or don't realize its importance for overall wellness.

2) Place your total scores for each Wellness Dimension Assessment on the corresponding section of the mobile. Because balance is such a critical aspect of overall well-being, compare your scores across the various dimensions.

How balanced are your dimensions of wellness?

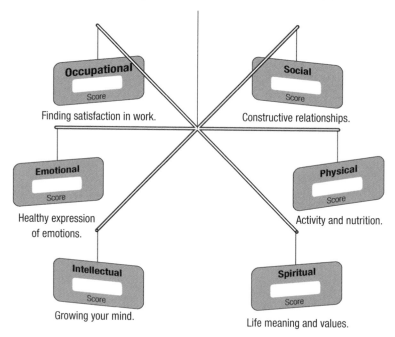

Occupational
Score
Finding satisfaction in work.

Social
Score
Constructive relationships.

Emotional
Score
Healthy expression of emotions.

Physical
Score
Activity and nutrition.

Intellectual
Score
Growing your mind.

Spiritual
Score
Life meaning and values.

(Graphic © 2008 Gorrow and Muller)

Attending to My Wellness

Week:

Striving for balance really is about what you value and how you prioritize your time. How will you balance your wellness this week? Choose one or two areas that need your attention and set goals for yourself.

Emotional:

Intellectual:

Occupational:

Physical:

Social:

Spiritual:

My action plan:

My visualization of success:

My reward:

References

AbuSabba, R., and C. Achterberg. 1997. Review of self-efficacy and locus of control for nutrition- and health-related behavior. *Journal of American Dietetic Association* 97(10): 1122–32.

American Association for Health Education/American Alliance for Health, Physical Education, Recreation and Dance. 2001. Report of the 2000 Joint Committee on Health Education and Promotion Terminology. *American Journal of Health Education* 32(2): 89–104.

American College of Sports Medicine and American Heart Association. 2007. *Guidelines for healthy adults under age 65.* Indianapolis, IN: ACSM.

Benson, H. 2003. *The breakout principle: How to activate the natural trigger that maximizes creativity, athletic performance, productivity and personal well-being.* New York: Simon & Schuster.

Blonna, R. 2007. *Coping with stress in a changing world*, 4th ed. New York: McGraw-Hill.

Bryner, J. 2006. Job stress fuels disease. *LiveScience*, November 22. Available at: *www.livescience.com/health/061122_job_stress.html.*

Calzadilla, R. 2008. 20 easy ways to burn 100 calories. *Gleemagazine.com*, April 4.

Cash, T. F., and T. Pruzinsky. 2002. *Body image: A handbook of theory, research, and clinical practice.* New York: Guilford Press.

Centers for Disease Control and Prevention. 2007. *BMI—Body mass index: About BMI for adults.* Atlanta, GA: CDC.

Charles, C. M. 2000. *The synergetic classroom: Joyful teaching and gentle discipline.* New York: Longman.

Conzemius, A., and J. O'Neill. 2006. *The power of SMART goals: Using goals to improve student learning.* Bloomington, IN: Solution Tree.

Culbert, H. 2006. Stress and efficiency: A little is good, a lot is not. *Wellness Works: Journey Towards Personal Wellness* 1(1): 32.

Dyer, W. W. 1976. *Your erroneous zones*. New York: Funk & Wagnalls.

Girdano, D. A., D. E. Dusek, and G. S. Everly Jr. 2005. *Controlling stress and tension*, 7th ed. San Francisco, CA: Pearson/Benjamin Cummings.

Goleman, D. 1995. *Emotional intelligence: Why it can matter more than IQ*. New York: Bantam Books.

Gorrow, T. R. 2004. Rearrange your attitude: The art of being happy. *Classroom Leadership* 8(1): 1, 6.

Gorrow, T. R., and S. M. Muller. 2008. Teacher retention: The three R's for interns. Presentation at the Maryland Professional Development School Conference, May 3, Owings Mills, MD.

Gorrow, T. R., S. M. Muller, and S. R. Schneider. 2005. The relationship between perceived body size and confidence in ability to teach among preservice teachers. *Education* 126(2): 364–73.

Hahn, D. B., W. A. Payne, and E. B. Lucas. 2007. *Focus on health*, 8th ed. Boston, MA: McGraw-Hill.

Hales, D. 2007. *An invitation to health*, 12th ed. Belmont, CA: Wadsworth.

Henderson, N., and M. M. Milstein. 2003. *Resiliency in schools: Making it happen for students and educators*, updated ed. Thousand Oaks, CA: Corwin.

Howley, E. T., and B. D. Franks. 2007. *Fitness professional's handbook*, 5th ed. Champaign, IL: Human Kinetics Publishers.

Insel, P. M., and W. T. Roth, eds. 2008. *Core concepts in health*, 10th ed. Boston: McGraw-Hill.

Karren, K. J., B. Q. Hafen, N. L. Smith, and K. J. Frandsen. 2006. *Mind/body health: The effects of attitudes, emotions, and relationships*, 3rd ed. San Francisco, CA: Benjamin Cummings.

Kramer, P. A., and Kappa Delta Pi. 2005. *The ABC's of classroom management: An A–Z sampler for designing your learning community.* Indianapolis, IN: Kappa Delta Pi, International Honor Society in Education.

Lefcourt, H. 2001. *Humor: The psychology of living buoyantly.* New York: Klewer Academic.

Lewine. H. 2005. The power of positive thinking. *Newsweek*, January 9. Available at: *www.newsweek.com/id/47991.*

National Sleep Foundation. 2007. *ABCs of zzzzs: When you can't sleep.* Washington, DC: NSF.

National Wellness Institute. 2007. The six dimensional model of wellness. Stevens Point, WI: NWI. Available at: *www.nationalwellness.org/index.php?id_tier=2&id_c=25.*

Ormrod, J. E. 2006. *Educational psychology: Developing learners*, 5th ed. Upper Saddle River, NJ: Merrill.

Romas, J. A., and M. Sharma. 2007. *Practical stress management: A comprehensive workbook for managing change and promoting health*, 4th ed. San Francisco, CA: Pearson/Benjamin Cummings.

Rosenfield, I. 1988. *The invention of memory: A new view of the brain.* New York: Basic Books.

Seaward, B. L. 2006. *Managing stress: Principles and strategies for health and well-being*, 5th ed. Sudbury, MA: Jones and Bartlett Publishers.

Seligman, M. E. P. 2002. *Authentic happiness: Using the new positive psychology to realize your potential for lasting fulfillment.* New York: Free Press.

Shearer, S., and L. Gordon. 2006. The patient with excessive worry. *American Family Physician* 73(6): 1049–56.

United States Department of Agriculture. 2007. Steps to a healthier weight. Washington, DC: USDA. Available at: *www.mypyramid.gov/steps/stepstoahealthierweight.html.*

Vandenberghe, R., and A. Huberman. 1999. *Understanding and preventing teacher burnout: A sourcebook of international research and practice*. Cambridge, MA: Cambridge University Press.

Warren, R. 2002. *The purpose driven life*. Grand Rapids, MI: Zondervan.

Wilcock, A. 2006. *An occupational perspective of health*, 2nd ed. Thorofare, NJ: Slack Inc.

Wild, B., M. Erb, M. Eyb, M. Bartels, and W. Grodd. 2003. Why are smiles contagious? *Psychiatry Research: Neuroimaging* 123(1): 17–36.

Wygand, J. W., and K. M. Cahill. 2006. Exercise programming. In *ACSM's certification review*, 2nd ed., ed. J. L. Roitman, K. W. Bibi, and W. R. Thompson, 154–72. Philadelphia, PA: Lippincott, Williams, & Wilkins.

Suggested Resources

American Academy of Family Physicians *www.familydoctor.org*

Anderson, G. 1995. *The 22 non-negotiable laws of wellness: Feel, think, and live better than you ever thought possible*. San Francisco: HarperCollins.

Anxiety Disorders Association of America *www.adaa.org.*

Gibbs, J. 2006. *Reaching all by creating Tribes learning communities*. Windsor, CA: CenterSource Systems.

Lundin, S. C., H. Paul, and J. Christensen. 2000. *FISH!* New York: Hyperion.

MentalHelp.net. 2004. Psychological self-tools, online self-help book. Available at: *http://mentalhelp.net/psyhelp*.

Travis, J., and R. S. Ryan. 2004. *Wellness index: A self-assessment of health and vitality*, 3rd ed. Berkeley, CA: Celestial Arts.

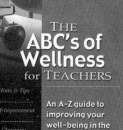

Kappa Delta Pi

International Honor Society in Education recognizes, supports, and provides resources for educational professionals throughout their careers.

Being involved in KDP is good for your professional well-being.

For Social Wellness, network with members across the globe.

Earn the Teacher of Honor recognition for Occupational Wellness.

To help support Emotional Wellness, launch an informal, local KDP chapter.

Write for KDP publications for your Intellectual Wellness.

To boost your wellness in several dimensions, get leadership experience on a national level: Review journal manuscripts, serve on a committee, or become a chapter counselor.

Learn more about what membership in Kappa Delta Pi can do for you: Go to *www.kdp.org*, call 800.284.3167, or e-mail *membership@kdp.org*.

An Honor to Join. A Benefit to Belong.

Attending to My Wellness

Week:

Striving for balance really is about what you value and how you prioritize your time. How will you balance your wellness this week? Choose one or two areas that need your attention and set goals for yourself.

Emotional:

Intellectual:

Occupational:

Physical:

Social:

Spiritual:

My action plan:

My visualization of success:

My reward:

Attending to My Wellness

Week:

Striving for balance really is about what you value and how you prioritize your time. How will you balance your wellness this week? Choose one or two areas that need your attention and set goals for yourself.

Emotional:

Intellectual:

Occupational:

Physical:

Social:

Spiritual:

My action plan:

My visualization of success:

My reward:

Notes